"The Golden Cobweb"

The Exotic Journey of an Englishman
who became Genealogist for the Thai Royal Family

BARBARA SCHOFIELD SULEIMAN

authorHOUSE

AuthorHouse™
1663 Liberty Drive
Bloomington, IN 47403
www.authorhouse.com
Phone: 833-262-8899

Published by AuthorHouse   07/11/2022

ISBN: 978-1-6655-6349-9 (sc)
ISBN: 978-1-6655-6348-2 (e)

Library of Congress Control Number: 2022911644

Print information available on the last page.

Any people depicted in stock imagery provided by Getty Images are models, and such images are being used for illustrative purposes only. Certain stock imagery © Getty Images.

This book is printed on acid-free paper.

JEFFREY FINESTONE:

Author. historian and genealogist, was born in Great Britain on 10th of May 1948.

He received his early training in genealogy at Burke's Peerage London, where he worked between 1972-1976.

His special area of study was the Royal Families of the World which he researched in depth.

He spent over a decade living in Thailand and Malaysia and passed away in Bangkok June 28th 1997.

*Jeffrey with one of the palace dance troupe in Java
during a royal wedding December 1990*

Beatrice is the narrator and as the story progresses the letters from her cousin Jeffrey take prominence. Initially full of optimism and joy they follow a tragic course and he died impoverished in Bangkok in 1997.

He left behind a body of work including two great works on the descendants of the Thai Royal family with much acclaim by King Bhumibol's sister, Her Royal Highness Princess Galyani Vadhana.

The letters span over 25 years and cover the essence of mid 20th century historical events.

Jeffrey's passion and dedication to his work is demonstrated throughout.

The Golden Cobweb

The cobweb glows golden illuminated by the rays of morning sun
Glimmering with its crystal drops of dew

Golden shimmers in the breeze
Capturing droplets of dew that glisten like crystal in the early
morning light
Danger lurks, sweeping away the beauty by a thoughtless hand

Contents

Chinese dragons

1

As he struggled with his final breaths, drifting in and out of a dimmed consciousness, thoughts fragmented, an awesome vision materialized floating over his ravaged body. An intricately carved dragon, scales gilded in gold with wings outstretched, clutched from its talons a magnificent chandelier. The myriad crystal drops glittered so brilliantly that they coalesced into a radiant cone of light amplified by the shimmering cascade of rubies spilling from a gaping fanged mouth and from the intensity of light emitted from multifaceted diamonds nesting in the eye sockets. Jeffrey's bleached sunken eyes, once a luminous cerulean, blinked at this dazzling display. Through parched lips he rasped inaudibly "let the sun shine in." The ghost of a smile graced his gaunt and ghastly features as he immersed himself into the final visualization of a precious life fully committing himself to eternity.

A letter, which he had been grasping in his hand, lay beside him as, with the infinite patience granted to the dead, he waited to be claimed by The Royal Family. The quiet side room with white washed walls overlooked the hospital grounds abundant with tropical vegetation. One wall bore a portrait of the King wearing a gold encrusted crimson jacket, who gazed down, through a pair of large spectacles, at the bed on which lay the prostrate body.

Through the narrow window Dawn entered, accompanied by the sound of awakening birds, throwing tentative rays of light onto the spotless marble floor. The day proceeded onwards until finally mid afternoon brought the appearance of the Princess fulfilling her ultimate obligation to this servant of the Court. She looked down at his spent body trying to recall his earlier beauty. Sighing, she muttered, "To honour my father I shall do this tiresome task."

When the princess had understood that Jeffrey was reaching the end of his long and arduous journey she had him transferred from his humble room north of Bangkok to King Chulalongkorn Memorial Hospital. He had been living in a nondescript building for the past few months, his last stop after progressive moves to lesser and lesser abodes mirroring his deterioration in health and financial resources.

The very day he was taken to the hospital a letter had arrived collected by the guard of the building. Tang was of uncertain age, his face deeply lined and skin leathery, a half-opened mouth displaying his few remaining teeth stained by betel nut. He sat on a frayed straw mat at the entrance, cross-legged, as he surveyed the comings and goings of his domain, a six-storey concrete block housing single rooms better described as cells, many of which were windowless. He had taken particular note of the poor foreigner when he had arrived a few months earlier clutching his cardboard box of scant belongings accompanied by a palace servant who had helped him up to the third floor. As lowly as was Tang, he ruled his territory imperiously. All visitors had to request his permission to enter the crumbling building. All letters and parcels were delivered into his care, which he then distributed with cautious responsibility ensuring that the rightful owners were made recipient. Nothing escaped his watchful eyes. Information was stored in his unhindered unschooled mind. He was aware of his power of observation knowing that it could serve him well one day.

On this particular day at midday the post arrived including a creased white envelope bearing a foreign stamp. It was recognized as Jeffrey's by virtue of the room number alone. Tang was illiterate but was proud of his ability to distinguish numbers. "This must be from his cousin in America," he thought remembering how the sick man had been aroused from increasing listlessness a couple of weeks before by such a letter. "My cousin has sent me money!" had shouted the foreigner with great joy.

The tuk tuk waited outside as Jeffrey descended the staircase more or less carried by the palace servant, the same man who had originally brought his charge to the building months before. As he passed by, Tang still sitting cross-legged on his mat stretched up with a graceful flexibility of sinewy arms and placed the envelope gently into the frayed pocket of Jeffreys' stained khaki trousers. "May the gods be with you," he said bowing discretely with hands clasped in front of his brow. "I will not be seeing him again," he said to himself, "may he leave this brutal cycle of life and reach Nirvana."

Childhood

2

J effrey appeared at the top of the staircase, disheveled curly blond hair framing an angelic face. Still in his pagamas, he stared incredulously down into the gloom of the dark wood paneled entrance hall, gripping onto to the narrow poles supporting the banister, too high for his reach. He was four years old but he already knew that he was the owner of the wooden rocking horse, which was parked below in a recess under a stained-glass window. Slanted shafts of light lit up dust beams. It was early morning and the house was in a slumber. All except for Jeffrey and, to his horror, his older cousin Beatrice just in the process of mounting his stead. "That is my horse," he shrilled as he hurtled down the carpeted stairs, "get off, get off immediately."

Beatrice had arrived the day before, deposited by her parents after traveling by train up the coast. It would be the first of many such excursions. Entering the vast entrance hall, a setting sun had illuminated the horse with a variegated mesh of moving colour as rays of light passed through the stained-glass panels: ecclesiastical purples, sky blues, deep magenta, ruby reds and saffron yellow, creating a magical halo. Impressively large, hewed out of oak, displaying a muscular body with a mane and arched tail of real hair, the stead was saddled and bridled with intricately worked leather, polished metal stirrups dangling from each side. An inviting glint of the amber glass eyes seemed to beckon to Beatrice alone to mount and ride off. The next morning, as dawn broke, she leapt out of bed oblivious of the thickly frosted window and clouds of breath emanating from her nostrils into the damp chilly bedroom. In flannel cotton nightdress she crept downstairs holding on tight to the wooden banisters. As she gathered up the reins and placed her foot on the stirrup she whispered "There, there." It was at that precise moment that Jeffrey flew down the staircase, face flushed with fury. There was much shoving, pushing and pulling. At first this battle was silent but both were indignant and they soon became more vocal. Beatrice was not going to relinquish her mount and Jeffrey was not going to concede. Her Aunt Freda appeared, in a rose-pink silk nightgown, the tall figure of authority. "Children" she said as firmly as she was capable with her gentle melodious voice, "you will wake up Robert." Jeffrey laughed maliciously. He did not care a damn if his baby brother woke up. He loathed him. Beatrice was contrite. She understood it was a grave offence to wake up babies. She dismounted, petted the wooden neck and regretfully intertwined her fingers through the rough mane, implanting a kiss at the level of the forelock. "I shall be back," she murmured. Jeffrey remained angry glaring viciously at his good-natured cousin. The aunt escorted them both back upstairs announcing that breakfast would be served in an hour assigning Betsy, the au pair, to dress them warmly. The aunt was slender and supple, refined facial features highlighted by accentuated cheeks, which maintained an unnatural high hue. Fine straight fair hair was shaped into a fashionable pageboy cut, the fringe dipping down towards watery blue eyes Her movements were graceful. Above all it was her voice that attracted one, soothing as honey.

By breakfast time the two cousins were giggling between bites of buttered toast, fingers sticky with homemade strawberry jam.

They became the best of friends and a few months later, early springtime, Jeffrey was looking forward to his cousin's impending arrival. Beatrice suffered from a chronic cough exacerbated by the prevailing smog, which afflicted the busy port city where she lived.

She was shipped off to St. Anne's whenever school holidays permitted to fill her soot filled lungs with pure ozone saturated sea air.

Picking up their unspoken camaraderie they waited for an opportune moment to slip away from the prying eyes of grown-ups. With winks and sly smiles, they crept out of the gloomy Victorian house venturing through a large unkempt garden, past the stately but rusted wrought iron gate guarded by a huge chestnut tree, which had already unfolded its umbrella-like foliage. Beatrice paused to reach up to the lowest lying branch. "Feel the sticky buds," she wheezed to her cousin who wondered what she was up to. "Do you play conkers?" Jeffrey was now getting impatient. He had no interest in sticky buds and no idea what conkers was except that it sounded rather silly. "Come on before Betsy catches us," he urged. Out on the unpaved road, habitually free of vehicles, cars still a rarity, they skipped about kicking up dust and knocking small pebbles out of their way. The first habitation they came across was a red brick home of more recent vintage. On the manicured front lawn a girl with freckled face, red hair tightly plaited into two long braids, waived to them. "Come and play," she lisped. Very soon the three of them became absorbed in play as if they had been buddies for years. But their concentration on serious play was interrupted by a high-pitched irritating voice calling the girl in for lunch. Their new friend turned to go but wavered, twisting around to face them. "Please come to my birthday party tomorrow afternoon," she asked in a grown-up formal manner clearly mimicking that of her parents.

Racing back to their own lunch they ran into the kitchen, which was presided over by Maude. Originally from the slums of Liverpool, Maude had been taken in by Aunt Freda early on in the war when her small council home by the docks had been bombed. Short in stature, stunted by chronic malnutrition, wearing huge National Health glasses with lenses as thick as pebbles, she peered at her hungry charges. With a toothless grin she placed a warm biscuit fresh out of the oven into each of their grimy hands, winking one of her gigantically magnified eyes. As they wolfed down their treats Betsy walked in. "Maude, what do you think you are doing?" Her voice was condescending. Turning to the children she grabbed them by the shoulders and marched them off to the kitchen sink scrubbing their hands impatiently. Her thoughts were elsewhere – her young man who was taking her that very evening to the Music Hall in Blackpool. In contrast to Maude's thin cotton dress, thread bare and faded from too many washes in harsh detergent, Betsy was smartly outfitted in her nanny uniform: a navy-blue affair with a pleated skirt and crisp white shirt sporting a well-knotted tie. Beatrice had noted other differences, which she had pondered over with perplexity: the way they spoke but especially their hands. Those of Maudes' were chaffed, reddened and coarse, with short permanently blackened fingernails. Betsy would sneer at poor Maude's hands. She would never allow that to happen to her. She spent hours "on my man-i-cure" as she proudly informed Jeffrey emphasizing each syllable as if it were a sign of her superiority, using a special wooden spatula to push down her cuticles, massaging a cream with great care into her plump smooth hands. This would be followed by an application of poster red nail polish which made Jeffrey's mother wince. Privately she would tell her sister that it made her nanny look rather like a lady of the streets. When Jeffrey heard this description of Betsy being enunciated to his aunt Marie, Beatrice's mother and confident of his mother, he puzzled over the significance of red nails and street ladies. "Now you may sit down for a proper lunch," she stated throwing a disdainful glance at Maude as she grabbed a small tray and sauntered off to the nursery where Robert partook of his repast separated safely from his hostile older brother. Maude fussed over her two charges. "Sit yer'selves down ye tzoo munkeys," she chided with affection. She plonked down the loaf of bread and a plate of tinned sardines arranged in neat rows glistening in a pool of oil. They sat at the wooden deal table perched on high stools their legs dangling, swinging back and forth with occasional furtive kicks underneath as they extracted freshly ironed napkins from individual bakelite serviette holders, identifiable by the etched pattern engraved around the side and the different swirls of colour. Slapping a generous spread of soft butter on thick slices of bread Maude urged "Eatz yer butties." As Jeffrey and

Beatrice chatted gaily about their invitation, Aunt Freda glided into the kitchen holding the hand of a silent toddler now two years old and still very much the bain of his older brother's otherwise perfect life. Jeffrey frowned at his mother and glared at Robert. "Oh Jeffrey," cooed his mother, "did you have a nice morning?" Her voice soothed his irritation and he excitedly related the adventure of meeting a new friend. His mother seemed pleased, blissfully unaware that they had broken the cardinal rule of not leaving the estate unattended. "We must find a nice present dear." Jeffrey jumped down from the stool and darted past Robert pinching his cheek thus setting off a round of crying from the bewildered child.

The next day a present had been construed: a prettily embroidered handkerchief, never used and still wrapped up in delicate tissue paper folded to show off some intricate embroidery of a butterfly on one corner. The aunt found plain buff wrapping paper in which her husband's most recent purchase from the Book Club had arrived. After lunch the children were put to work. They were to decorate the paper with stenciled flowers, colouring with wax pencils. Bearing the gift, the wrapping paper totally covered in a riot of colour and tied with a satin ribbon, they were allowed to walk down the road by themselves as long as Beatrice held onto Jeffrey's hand. Out of sight of his doting mother, as soon as they rounded the bend, he quickly extricated himself from this obligation and pranced ahead in excited anticipation. A gaggle of noisy happy children spilled out from the house into the garden. A man in a tweed suit was on all fours on the lawn playing with his daughter perched on his back waving merrily at her arriving guests. This enthusiastic welcome did not stop the mustachioed father from glaring at them suspiciously with piercing brown eyes. "What are you two doing here?" he barked, looking at them as if they were ragamuffins. "We are invited," answered Beatrice, still optimistic that the father would realize his mistake and extend a warm reception. He slowly stood up after depositing his daughter down, taking his time to brush off some soil clinging to his neatly pressed trousers, before snarling, "Not by me, you haven't. You are not allowed in. Be off." A shame welled up in both of them, and with bowed heads and leaden legs they returned in silence, tears obscuring their vision. With Beatrice still clutching onto the present, Jeffrey had silently reached up to grasp the other hand of his cousin. The house was quiet when they entered. Eventually the mother appeared and without a word she reclaimed the present looking pensive but did not venture to ask what had occurred. No one said anything, no discussion was undertaken to explain this brutal behaviour. Uncle Stanley was tucked away upstairs in a quiet room as was his habit to nurse the migraines which often plagued him. The angry face of the man haunted them. They remained silent the rest of the day. Only Maude took notice of the two gloomy faces. She tweaked the story from them prompting another round of tears from Beatrice. "Don't yer wury ye tzoo poomkins abouzt 'im, the bestard," she said hugging them to her bony chest from which Jeffrey wriggled free. That evening Beatrice found the handkerchief lying carelessly on her bed. She gave it to Maude. At six years of age she felt something had changed in how she viewed the world. She felt less safe.

Days of driving incessant rain, with low hung dark clouds pressing down over sodden soil, and with vast puddles undulating under the force of a chilling wind, any ideas of outdoor adventure were vanquished. They were housebound. The attic was next on the list of conquests. Sternly forbidden to venture up there, the two plotted their course one particularly dark dreary day when the wind rattled the windows and the rain fell in heavy sheets. The parents always took a nap in the afternoon after lunch. Betsy was claimed in the nursery where Robert harboured a cold and Maude was engrossed in scrubbing pots, a self-imposed chore which she performed ritualistically once a month fervently polishing them to a state of newness.

Jeffrey was quite a solemn child when not provoked into an irrational anger, which could progress rapidly into a full-blown tantrum. His parents had noted that when his cousin came to stay the house was far more tranquil and that the object of his wrath, Robert, was greatly lessened. Now the two of them were intent on their adventure. Beatrice had been daydreaming about a hidden treasure tucked away in the forbidden domain, which shored up her courage to tackle the dark back staircase with Jeffrey in tow. They padded up the stairwell in bare feet clinging tight with arms outstretched to grasp the next steep step without making too much noise although some creaking could not be avoided. At the top, in almost complete darkness, they found the door into the attic ajar. A musty odour pervaded this vast space barely illuminated by a series of porthole windows along the sloping eaves. The panes of glass were almost obscured by a thick layer of dust dimming the already dull light from outdoors. Huge silhouettes of armoires and shelves loomed out at them. As their eyes adjusted Beatrice, apprehensive to find themselves wrapped in a blanket of silence, tried to distract herself by rummaging in a trunk which had spilled out its contents of old clothes in an array around it. "Jeffrey, this is where the treasure is kept," she whispered. Jeffrey did not reply. He had made his way to a pile of books. Unable to read he was nonetheless captivated by a book with images of well-dressed ladies and gentlemen. He sat down on the floor and with great concentration and furrowed brow slowly turned each page and carefully focused on each picture. He was not to be disturbed. Beatrice dug out a box containing necklaces and rings. She was content. Deciding her goal had been achieved it was time to leave. Thick cobwebs draped in odd corners and strange squeaks took precedence over her curiosity. Jeffrey had remained absorbed the whole time and when she tugged at his sleeve he sighed and tucked the book under his arm to take downstairs.

Safely back in the drawing room where Maude had lit a coal fire in the ample fireplace, they sunk back, side by side, on a worn leather sofa and reviewed their finds. Jeffrey shoved the book under his cousin's nose pointing with a grubby finger at one particular page, which fascinated him. Beatrice, proud of her ability to read sounded out "Queen Victoria in Windsor Castle knitting." It was a photograph of the queen in her dotage, plump and pasty faced, a lace cap on her head, sitting with a younger woman in an ornate drawing room crowded with paintings on the wall, vases and small objects on tables and mantelpieces, dominated by a candled chandelier. He was captivated. "Is that our Queen?" he questioned. Beatrice wasn't sure. She thought they had a king but maybe it was his wife.

—⚉—

Two months later Jeffrey was chauffeured to Liverpool for a very special event. Beatrice had been right: they did have a king but he had since died and now the new queen was to be crowned. For the first time, this historical event was to be viewed by all those fortunate to possess or have access to a new electronic device, the television. The week before, Beatrice had been picked up early from school by her father enthusiastic to show off this exotic contraption of modernity. Placed ostentatiously in the middle of their otherwise neat dining room, a box sat on a low stool with wires protruding at odd angles and an inflexible length of unseemly antennae perched on top like a giant insect. Her father fiddled clumsily with a number of knobs and anxiously twisted around the antennae. The blank screen began to quiver with life as a series of horizontal black and white lines appeared jumping nervously up and down representing the state of mind of her father. He stood back enthralled, lost in reverie. Beatrice crept out unnoticed to play rounders with her friends at the top of the road, a cul-de-sac.

On the day in question, all the families in the road were invited to their home, being the only house possessing this machine. Beatrice had been up early helping her mother prepare a mountain of sandwiches, spreading egg mayonnaise or tinned salmon paste over the buttered slices of bread. "Not too much Beatrice," her mother admonished, as she aligned the top slice of white bread, cutting off the crusts which were consumed rapidly by her and her older sister Janet. The tea trolley groaned under the weight of these sandwiches and homemade cakes and biscuits. An aunt and uncle appeared, cousins in tow, and soon the lounge, the new shrine for the revered object, was crammed with visitors. It was to be a long day. Sitting quietly, cross-legged in his grey flannel shorts and starched white shirt with a perfectly knotted tie was Jeffrey, nose almost touching the flickering screen. Mesmerized, he did not budge, nibbling distractedly at an occasional sandwich. His future was decided on that very day. The Coronation was decisive and an unwavering obsession and devotion to royalty was born. Centuries of royal protocols had evolved into a dazzling display of ritual enhanced with armies of liveried members of the vast royal household. A slow procession of innumerable ornate carriages accompanied by mounted escorts led the way from Buckingham Palace to the Westminster Abbey carrying Heads of State, nobles and Foreign Royals. At last appeared Her Majesty's Procession led by the Household Cavalry, The Foot Guards, the Band and Corps of Drums of the Welsh and Irish Guards, the King's troop and Royal Horse Artillery. The State Coach, gilded in gold, pulled by eight grey prancing horses wearing red Moroccan harness led by riders walking alongside concluded this triumphal march. The Abbey glittered with the jewels of Lords and Ladies of the realm. The Sovereign to be crowned entered, assisted by six maids of honour carrying the six-yard long Robe of State of crimson velvet edged in ermine and two rows of embroidered gold lace. As the ceremony proceeded Jeffrey fretted for the young queen. Picking up from the commentator's description of the weight of the crown he turned to his aunt "poor lady, how can she carry that hat, she will get a headache." No one answered his fraught concerns.

—〰—

Two years had passed by when Jeffrey was packed off to Boarding School. Between his mother's fragile state, his father's chronic migraines and his own undying hate of his younger brother, the decision was hardly soul searching. A large cardboard box filled with carefully scissored articles on his beloved royal family accompanied the large shiny metallic school trunk. Leaving behind a tearful Robert with Betsy and Maude, Jeffrey sat ensconced between his taciturn parents in their ancient Rover with its scuffed leather seats, driven by the faithful retainer Charlie. Dropped off at Lime Street station in Liverpool they were to board the overnight train to London. Unaware of his impending abandonment, Jeffrey shuddered at the vision of grime and the onslaught of unaccustomed noise presented by this old Victorian station. Dwarfed by the arching iron girders soaring overhead, the grey light of outside further dimmed by the impenetrability of more than a century of accumulated dirt adhering tenaciously to the glass panes of a once glorious ceiling, the family remained silent. The porter led the way, pushing their luggage piled onto a wooden cart, past the monstrous steam fueled engine down the long platform. He was a thin wiry man, wearing a modest uniform frayed at cuffs and trouser-bottoms, cap perched jauntily on the side of his head. "Wur's you goin yung lad?"he spluttered displaying a toothless grin. Jeffery turned away in disdain, already aware of the divisions in society. Besides he wasn't really sure where he was in fact going. His mother looked especially pretty wearing a waisted dress cut on the bias with a floral print, the mid-calf hem highlighting her slender legs covered in fine silk stockings with the back seams perfectly aligned. His father looking stern, a trilby hat covering his wiry hair, wore a thick tweed wool jacket hanging carelessly over his slight frame, a bow tie giving the final touch to his checkered shirt. They climbed up steep metal steps to enter the first-class carriage, edged their way down the narrow corridor and found their compartment. "Reserved" muttered Jeffrey, reading aloud the faded black letters on a yellowed card affixed in the brass slot next to the sliding doors. A young man formally introduced himself as their attendant. "I'll be back to make your beds Madam," he said addressing only the mother. Jeffrey perked up. "Where are the beds?" "You will see darling," said his mother looking distracted with her habitual expression of concern tinged with an inexplicable sadness. Night was falling, dimming further the gloomy station. They settled down sinking into the plush velvet seats, Jeffrey sitting by the window intent on observing the jostling crowds wearing drab clothes lugging scuffed battered suitcases as they filed past his window to the second-class carriages. "What is the difference mummy?" he queried. "They will be sitting up all night," she answered sighing as she imagined their discomfort.

Amidst the clattering of trolleys and the raucous shouts of the porters a whistle sounded. A sudden explosion of sound startled Jeffrey as his eyes opened wide with fear. It was the loudest noise he had ever heard. "Is that a bomb!" he shouted. He had been born after the Great War not far from the worst bombing efforts of the enemy. Inevitably the war stories of his aunts and uncles had penetrated his conscious, capturing his imagination fostering a horror of destruction. His father aroused himself from his usual state of introspection and led him out of the compartment to stand at the open door of the carriage. "Look!" he ordered, a command barely heard through the cacophonous eruptions of white steam spewed out in bursts from the engine and coughed up with great force towards the high vaulted ceiling amplified by repetitive echoes. A conductor walked with grim determination down the platform slamming the doors shut. On returning to their compartment the attendant arrived with an armful of clean cotton sheets and warm wool blankets. He cracked jokes as he converted the seats to beds pulling down the top bunk for Jeffrey. "Thought it wer the krauts did yer, yung lad eh?" he cackled. The train jerked out of the station, past rusting girders of steel, slowly gaining speed as it chugged past by the rows of council houses interspersed by heaps of rubble, the bomb sites yet to be cleared. As it rattled over the bridge spanning the River Mersey, a rocking rhythm augmented by the clicking of the steel rail connections at regular intervals, became hypnotic. Jeffrey could no longer fight the fatigue induced by the excitement of the day.

They arrived in London, an early September morning with clear skies and just a tinge of autumnal chill. A cab conveyed them to Brown's Hotel in Mayfair. Aunt Freda would not consider anywhere else worthy of her visit. Unaware of her elder son's dreams and yearnings she had chosen well, being the hotel known to many foreign royals. It was also the place that grandees and members of parliament stayed when in town from their country estates to participate in the important business of running the country. The spacious lobby and lounge was slightly decrepit, harbouring ancient stuffed leather sofas worn out with cracks and tears, threadbare Persian carpets and a pervasive odour of cigar smoke and spilled whisky which permeated the air. Upkeep had been abandoned for more important matters during the war and its aftermath. Men, variously whiskered or not sat in groups, whispering amongst themselves no doubt in preparation for some important political announcement. Jeffrey felt immediately at ease. "I like it here Mummy," he announced happily, beaming, unusual for his normal countenance of furrowed brow and stern watchful eyes. "Is this my school?" "No darling, we have another journey tomorrow."

Being close to Bond Street Jeffrey was taken shopping by his mother while his father stayed in the hotel room already in pygamas propped up with a nest of pillows on the comfortable bed reading the newspaper, thin-rimmed tortoiseshell glasses perched at the end of his nose.

Despite evident destruction from the wartime bombing and the general population still looking a bit worse for wear, there was a breeze of optimism brewing. Rationing had finally been banished so their first task was to fill up Jeffreys' tuck box. They stopped off at Fortnum and Masons. Assailed by mouthwatering displays of enormous jars of candies they were flummoxed. After careful consideration the newly acquired wooden box was filled with a variety of toffees, fudge, pear drops, liquorices and chocolates. The shop girl looked at the little boy standing in front of the counter appearing so serious and rather forlorn and could not resist leaning over the counter to ruffle his hair. "Don't do that!" he shouted, recoiling from her touch. She winked at his mother and mouthed, "he must be rather nervous." The mother gave an embarrassed smile and nodded. Unperturbed by the boys' reaction she showed Jeffrey a variety of satin ribbons and asked him to choose the colour. At this he gave a wan smile and pointed to the scarlet ribbon. Armed with a large box heavy with delicacies. wrapped in the store's colourful paper bound by a huge scarlet bow, Jeffrey walked out slowly onto the London street feeling very proud. They passed by a milliners. His mother's gaze lingered on a blond mink hat with a silk chocolate brown tassel dangling to one side. It was displayed prominently in the window. "Oh Mummy, do try that on," urged Jeffrey. An extravagant purchase was made. His mother always wore that very hat on the rare occasions she would visit the school in the ensuing years, regardless of the season. The next day they left for Victoria Station. The cab drove slowly down The Mall prolonging Jeffrey's first view of Buckingham Palace. His heart palpated violently against his thin chest, as he trembled with excitement, imagining his beloved royals participating in their daily rituals.

They boarded the Brighton Belle; a much quieter experience since this famous train was electric. Jeffrey could not make out whether or not this journey was a joyous occasion. Inside the handsome Pullman carriage with marquetry panels, brass fittings and table lamps glowing under handmade lampshades, he removed his new school cap, grey wool with brick red lettering spelling out the name of his new school "Whittinghame College." He placed it solemnly on the seat next to him. His grey wool jacket, with the school's crest embroidered on the top pocket, almost reached his knees covering the short trousers. He examined his bare exposed knees, glistening in the yellow light of the brass lamp on the table, contemplating the day in the far-off future when he would be grown up enough to wear long trousers. His mother leaned over to straighten his school tie patterned with red and white diagonal stripes.

The Beacons

The tight knit Beacon Family harboured many secrets, most unvoiced merely hinted. Sometimes an unwieldly secret escaped the bondage of silence and demonstrated its presence in broad daylight.

Cousin Robin made his first appearance at Jeffrey's barmitzvah. He was the first son of Joanne, youngest of three glamorous sisters, whose parents contributed to the war effort by entertaining American officers from the military base outside Liverpool. Barely a teenager, Joanne moved freely amongst the army officials learning quickly the power of her beauty. Whiskey flowed copiously and a cigarette haze in their home competed with the smog outside. Rationing cards were not needed. Their war was 'a good one' as some fortunates were able to express. Midway through the world conflagration the youngest son of the Beacons, Peter, a newly minted lawyer, recently called up to serve his country, fell helplessly in love with the teenage Joanne. Against all protestations of family and community a quick wartime marriage ensued before he was shipped off to North Africa. Robin was conceived and born to the sounds of German firebombs whistling through the low cast clouds, launched in great profusion, to land on the rooftops and back yards of the Liverpudlians. On an unannounced leave from the theatre of war, young Peter flushed with excitement at the thought of seeing his gorgeous wife and infant boy, burst into their small semidetached home newly built outside the city in a village called Childwall. Joanne had done herself proud towards helping the allied cause, offering her ample embraces to lonely servicemen and Peter arrived during one of these war efforts.

The court awarded Robin to the care of his maternal grandparents. Peter returned broken hearted to the front only to find that the war was over. Joanne sailed blissfully through many more embraces before finding the next unsuspecting husband blinded by her shimmering sophisticated allure.

Two husbands later Joanne swept up North to collect her son and dutifully enrolled him in her husband's alma mater down in Surrey. This elite boarding school was snobby and cruel to outsiders. Then Joanne died suddenly of unknown cause. Robin set off to London to attend Art School and promptly had a massive nervous breakdown. At the age of 21 he was returned to his maternal grandparents up North.

Meanwhile, from his school in the South of England, Jeffrey was dictating the details desired for his religious coming of age. Only the Hotel Majestic in his seaside home of Lythm St. Annes would do. It was a famed Edwardian extravaganza. If it was good enough for Churchill then it certainly passed muster with Jeffrey. All the Beacons were to assemble there for the weekend; the menu and drinks were rigidly elucidated and his flustered mother had to negotiate with the officiating rabbi about what was permissible without upsetting her son.

At Easter Vacation Jeffrey swept into his home, now a spacious bungalow near the centre of St. Annes, to ensure that his requests had been met. Robert cowered in his bedroom. When he emerged for meals he remained mute since during his older brother's visits his stutter was so prominent he was rendered unintelligible. Robert too had been packed off to boarding school but at one a great distance from Jeffrey's. His older brother was oblivious to such an insignificant presence.

It was a warm spring, the air saturated with the fragrance of apple blossoms and lilac: an auspicious backdrop for the festivities. The clan gathered in the vast entrance hall of the grand hotel clustered in groups chattering vivaciously amongst themselves. If one mustered courage to eavesdrop much of the chitchat circled around the imminent arrival of the forsaken cousin Robin. Jeffrey clucked with delight at the sight of gigantic aspidistras in huge Chinese porcelain pots placed in darkened corners and he positively gasped in admiration of the stately staircase fanning out onto the mosaic-marbled floor. Bronze statues of women in flowing gowns and garlanded heads graced each side of the staircase at the bottom of the gleaming ebony banisters.

A brief silence descended as all turned to examine the newcomer. He was short, pale and pasty with sparse wispy dirty blond hair, a high forehead above protruding globular eyes of washed out blue. A cloak of loneliness enveloped him. His father pretended not to see him. Accompanied by his aunt Beryl, the older sister of his deceased mother Joanne who had also migrated home after a wild life in the States, he boldly introduced himself. His speaking voice was confident, self-assured, belying his underlying weakness, with a perfectly modulated Public School boy accent. Beatrice whispered in Jeffrey's ear "who is he?" She had not been aware of the preceding gossip surrounding his return to the Beacon fold. "But is he a real cousin?" asked cousin Stephen. "Of course he is" said Jonathen his younger brother, wise beyond his years. "But why didn't we know we had another cousin?" voiced Beatrice again, upset that such an important fact had eluded them all.

As they were ushered into the renowned tea-room, ornate with a glass vaulted ceiling soaring high above and more potted palms scattered around the periphery, Beatrice and Jeffrey fell into conversation with Robin. They were both enamoured by his distinguished manner. And once Beatrice uncovered the fact that he was also an avid horseman, all doubts on his provenance evaporated. Jeffrey and Beatrice accepted him totally, embracing his strangeness of manner, impressed with his red convertible sports car with its Corp Diplomatic license plates and above all his quiet aristocratic manner.

Neighbours

4

Aunt Freda determined that Jeffrey would become a partner in her older brothers' law firm "Beacon & Beacon." Uncle Peter was a barrister and his brother Arthur was a solicitor. They made a good team; Peter was flamboyant, always mildly inebriated, erudite in court taking on infamous cases of the day. Arthur, wearing wire rim glasses and well-cut suits looked severe and highly professional.

Over the winter break from his first year at Liverpool University Jeffrey turned up in the Chelsea flat on Oakley Street where his cousin Beatrice lived after graduating from London University. She was completing an apprenticeship at St Thomas' Hospital none too happy with her chosen path but soldiering on.

A ray of sunshine appeared at the door. "Jeffrey!" she shrieked throwing herself at him to embrace her most beloved friend. Together they drank up the intoxicating whirl of the late 60's: drinks at the local Markham pub, supper at the Chelsea Kitchen, dancing at the Pheasantry club which buzzed with budding celebrities and hanging out with Beatrice's eclectic group of friends. The highlight of his stay was entertaining the cast of "Hair" in her flat. "How do you know them?"

"Oh, I auditioned for a part last week," he answered not at all crestfallen that he had been rejected, after all now they were all partying together. The actors adored him and he was in his element.

But the night before returning up North Jeffrey was morose. Through clenched teeth he moaned, "I absolutely loathe Law, I hate it." Twirling around the room he stamped his feet in anger reminiscent of his tantrums when he was a child. "But Jeffrey, whatever you do or plan to do please, please finish the course." She tried to find the right phrases to explain the importance of having a profession. Beatrice herself had gone through four years of anguish having realized she should have gone to medical school, which she had foolishly renounced. "You may even find a way of enjoying it. Look, I find pharmacology fascinating and who knows, ---." She didn't finish since she had no idea how she could find satisfaction herself with her qualifications.

Her cousin was unmoved by her protestations. He departed in a dark mood.

A month later he was her neighbour, close by on a small side street off the Kings Road. On the train back to Liverpool he had been robbed. "Beatrice," he drawled in barely suppressed delight, as he lounged on a well-worn couch in his bedsit, "The suitcase with all my law notes was stolen. A clear sign of my destiny don't you think?" Aunt Freda did not think that at all. She even believed her niece Beatrice was an accomplice in this rash act, a bad influence. Ever since living in the capital city where they have "funny ideas," she hinted to Beatrice's mother of this nefarious influence. Her mother didn't defend her since she too disapproved of the path of independence her daughter had taken. But in keeping with the family ethos no words were spoken.

Jeffrey had no intention of being supported by his parents. He took on temporary clerical jobs and was finally hired by Burke's Peerage to write updates on the Royal Families of Europe. "Beatrice, I was in the London Times today!" She was suitably impressed. "Yes, I was waiting outside the Westminster Abbey to await for the Queen's Opening of Parliament and my opinion was requested by a reporter." He had been validated and a cutting of the article was sent to his parents in the hope they would join in his enthusiasm.

One day Jeffrey arrived to her flat in a state of feverish excitement. He could barely speak. "She nodded to me!" "Who nodded to you?" "The Dowager Princess Alice of course," spluttered Jeffrey, beside himself with the honour bestowed on him. Every Sunday since his arrival in London he had attended her church in Knightsbridge, and finally she had noticed him, discretely inclining her head in his direction.

From the New Year of 1970 until August of that very same year the two cousins cavorted around London in a whirlwind of youthful energy.

"My dear Beatrice, next Saturday at midday I will meet you at the entrance of Westminster Abbey at 2pm. You must be dressed elegantly and you may not ask me any questions. I have a surprise for you." It was late spring and as Beatrice crossed over Westminster Bridge from her work at St. Thomas' Hospital she pondered over his precise instructions. At the exact proposed time a taxi drew up carrying Jeffrey who beckoned her in. She watched him pass on a folded piece of paper to the taxi driver who turned around in surprise after reading the directive. The weather was splendid, the blossoms in full bloom emanating a delicate fragrance which wafted about in the gentle breeze. As the taxi proceeded towards The Mall, Beatrice's excitement grew. "Hey, Jeffrey, we are not going to have tea with the Queen are we?" she joked half hoping her cousin could pull off such a feat. He remained silent staring ahead intently. They had arrived at the Palace gates where a gaggle of tourists hung out in anticipation of royal arrivals. The taxi driver leaned out of his window and handed the note to the palace guard. The gates parted slowly and they inched forward as Beatrice's heart thumped wildly. They came to a stop in front of the main doors and Jeffrey, still impenetrable in his silence, helped his trembling cousin out of the taxi. He steered her to the right to an adjacent door and knocked using the heavy ornate knocker. A stern-faced footman in palace livery listened gravely to Jeffrey's request and ushered them in. Down a simple corridor they were escorted to the Privy Room where an imposing desk held a huge embossed leather-bound book. It was the Guest Book. A velvet armrest was provided and an ink pen placed next to it. Jeffrey signed first and then his cousin.

They were shown the way out and as they started to walk across the vast courtyard to the Palace Gates, the tourists clustered closer behind the railings snapping away with the cameras.

Dazed, they walked to the park, Jeffrey as thrilled as Beatrice. "How?" asked Beatrice. Now animated, his plan pulled off, Jeffrey explained, "All the Queen's subjects are permitted this honour but no one knows about it. Isn't that amazing?" They linked arms laughing about their exhilarating adventure.

Working for Burke's Peerage gave Jeffrey entrée to numerous official events and he would take his cousin as his escort, the Honourable Mrs. Jeffrey Finestone. When the Crown Prince of Laos came for a State Visit, Jeffrey dragged Beatrice for a test run the day before to ensure they would arrive in time for the event at the Laotian Embassy in Kensington Park. On the day in question Jeffery quivered with delight, "Oh Beatrice, I have never seen so many royal members at one time" referring to the six grown children. Her cousin gazed at her in pride as she conversed in French with the Crown Prince.

Afternoon tea with Jeffrey became a Saturday ritual with certain rules strictly enforced. Entering the charmingly furnished haven of his bedsit she was admonished for requesting coffee. "My dear cousin, you have been invited for tea, and please refrain from smoking. I loathe the smell of smoke." A magnificent porcelain tea set had been laid out on a small table made of darkly varnished paper-mâché inlaid with mother of pearl. The tea set was part of a complete dinner service acquired at the age of eight when the eldest sister of their mothers, Aunt Baile, an avid collector of objects d'arte, had taken him to an auction. Besotted by the patterned porcelain he had bidden for the whole set. Over a cup of fragrant tea and nibbling on biscuits arranged artfully on small side plates they exchanged stories. Conversation was richly peppered with anecdotes of royal misdemeanors. Jeffrey allowed Beatrice to review parts of the masterpiece he was writing in honour of the Queen's Silver Jubilee planned for 1977. It was to be a complete history of British Royalty. Beatrice noted his distinctive writing style and she always looked forward each Saturday to reading the drafts.

Early summer brought the appearance of Robin to their doorsteps. He was in town for the highlight of Royal Ascot. Mysterious about his lodgings he did accept the Saturday tea at Jeffrey's flat. Before taking his seat at the tea table he poised a moment before announcing "My dear cousins I have badges for both of you to join me in the Royal Enclosure." Both gasped at this unexpected invitation, not quite believing it could be possible. The exclusivity of entering the Royal Enclosure was a well-known fact and even with Jeffrey's London connections he had not even dared to dream of being so close to his beloved Royal family. Robin explained, "My stepfather, as you know, is an honoured member." They didn't know.

Finally, the day came. Beatrice had changed her work schedule. Her colleagues were most accommodating and demanded a full report of the event. She borrowed a wide brimmed hat from her close friend Sonia, an actress. "My darling you look absolutely marvelous in this one," she had said handing Beatrice a dramatic piece, which was indeed most suitable. Jeffrey rented a grey morning suit with top hat. They were picked up outside Beatrice's flat by Robin at the wheel of his red sports car, looking exceptionally dapper. They set off for Great Windsor Park under a deep blue cloudless sky with temperatures soaring: a perfect day. They parked carelessly at the edge of the Great Lawn, already carpeted with the fine linens of different picnic parties. A gentle hum of contentment and anticipation filled the air. From the trunk of their car, with its diplomatic license plates, emerged a straw hamper filled with sandwiches from Fortnum and Mason and a silver ice-filled bucket bearing a bottle of champagne. Barely had they finished the picnic and sipping the last drops of champagne, Jeffrey glanced at his watch. Startled he shouted out "Good grief, I shall miss the Royal Procession!" He was referring to the carriage ride bearing the royal party from Windsor Castle, which circulated the racetrack signaling the start of the races for that day. Looking up from the red tartan wool blanket, upon which Robin reclined languidly, he answered, "Oh my dear boy, we have plenty of time." "No we don't!" shrieked Jeffrey his face now contorted with concern, suffused with a bright crimson hue of anger. Without further ado he bolted towards the racetrack. Then Robin slowly stood up, adjusted his top hat, and without a word sauntered off and disappeared among the gathering crowds converging in the same direction. Beatrice had been abandoned, her handbag locked in the car and no badge or any identification for that matter. "What will I tell Sonia, the people at work, all my friends?" She surveyed the scene. A multitude of people, the majority of whom milled around the fences, were dressed casually in jeans and T-shirts. "The plebeians," she muttered to herself disdainfully. Forcing her way through the throngs she passed by huge tents, set up for different groups, boisterous people clustered inside, drinks in hand. In one particular tent a television set had been placed on top of a box and a group of men were avidly cheering for a cricket game. The sun was beginning to beat down relentlessly. A friendly policeman gave her directions to the gate for the Royal Enclosure. Once there, the policeman on guard gazed impassively as she gulped out her story: "I have lost my cousins one of whom has my badge. Could you please overhead page him?" "I don't know if that be done 'ere me lady," he replied indifferently. She was so genuinely distressed he took pity and pointed out, beyond the gate, a small tent. "Maybe's they can 'elp." Inside the coolness of the tent sat three young girls no doubt, in Beatrice's mind, the debutantes of the season. They stared at her coldly searching for a name tag to ascertain whether or not she was titled and thus worthy of their attention. With nothing to lose Beatrice took her stance and as haughtily as she could muster uttered "Would you please look over the guest list for my cousins' name?" She was not sure if there was such a list and worse she was beginning to doubt if Robin even had access himself. But her determination was powerful and exasperated by her insistence one of the girls announced icily "I shall have a policeman escort you until you find your cousin." Her escort was young and courteous, listening to her true story of woe: Robin was nowhere to be seen, she had missed seeing the Queen being driven in her open horse pulled carriage, and now what? From some inner resource, she found herself requesting to walk down to the fence to watch the race "Since I have placed a bet and I want to watch closely." Smiling, the policeman waved her off "Hope you find your young man miss."

The afternoon wore on with occasional forays into the long low building which housed the bar trying to discern through dense clouds of cigar smoke whether her cousin was there.

After the last race, with sun setting, she joined the mass of guests exiting through the main gate, dragging her feet feeling sorry for herself especially after encountering a group of people she actually knew; the Nicaraguan ambassador and his large brood whom she had met at one of the events with Jeffrey. Some pleasantries were exchanged and she cursed the fact that she hadn't spotted them earlier. Heading back to the Park she sighted the two of them walking together. Robin was absolutely indifferent to the fact that they had been separated. No explanation was given and no inquiry offered as to her welfare. Jeffrey, on the other hand, was triumphant. "Beatrice" he spluttered, flecks of saliva at the corner of his mouth, which always occurred when he was highly excited, "I now know how the Queen Mother keeps cool!" He continued, oblivious of his cousins' distress, "She has a small handkerchief passed to her by her lady in waiting and mops her brow discretely. I stood right next to her." This detail of royal day-to-day life was manna to him. "Do you know I paid eight pounds for the Tattersalls adjoining the Royal Enclosure. And what do you know —one has access to the Royal Paddock where the horses are cooled down after each race, and that," he continued, "is where she was petting one of her horses."

It was now dusk and the shadows lengthened, light dimming as the trees loomed over the parked cars silhouetted by the setting sun. A delicious cool breeze enveloped them. Jeffrey did not want his joy diluted by her anger against Robin: and so it was.

—⟋w⟍—

A month later they mapped out their different destinies. Beatrice set off to France to join an avant-guarde theatre group. Jeffrey's involvement in royal affairs deepened.

Separation

After a year had passed by Beatrice was back in London working at a temporary job for a few weeks, staying in her former flat on Oakley Street with obliging flatmates. She had returned earlier from her adventure with theatre and was living at home in Liverpool journeying down to London each weekend suffering a brutal affair with an unworthy man. Jeffrey was her bollard of sanity. The relationship was finally ended and now, back in her beloved city for this prolonged period of time, she would take her cousin with her to hang out at the Chelsea Arts Club. She was probably the only non-artist allowed access, although Ley Kenyon the President of the club and a former lover was proud of her foray into theatre. Ley took a special interest in Jeffrey. "What an unusual family you are," he would say as they all sat at the bar with its remarkable backdrop of a trompe l'oeil mural depicting messages on a board, deceptively real. On her days off work the two cousins would sit in the unkempt but quiet and spacious garden behind the club reading papers and catching up with delicious stories.

At the end of three weeks and before departing for Europe to visit friends, Beatrice decided to take up an offer to stay the weekend in Brighton. Ramon had been at boarding school with Jeffrey and, since his mother had opened a business there, he stayed on. Now he was living with Jackie and both were delighted to entertain anyone related to Jeffrey.

As her cousin was otherwise engaged, Beatrice made her way alone taking an early train. Walking up the hill from the station under a cloudless sky she determined that she would give up on men, for the time being at least, and concentrate on her own needs. Greeted effusively by her hosts and, with lunchtime looming, a picnic in the garden was in order. "Let's invite Farid," suggested Beatrice. "Of course, of course," the couple chimed in unison, "we all had so much fun last year." They were referring to a gathering the previous summer year of alumni of the Whittinghame College. Farid, one such alumnus, had also remained in Brighton when his family had joined him from Iraq.

A tablecloth was laid out on the lawn as a distant chime announced the arrival of their guest. Beatrice ran to the door. Farid, a neat conservatively dressed young man sporting a brilliant white starched open necked shirt, pressed trousers and shining black leather shoes was accompanied by a distressed, bearded man with a halo of black curls cascading down to his shoulders, wearing a torn jean jacket covering a tightly fitted wrinkled faded flowery lilac shirt. It was her future husband, Sami!

Sami had just landed in London from New York and was staying with his cousins, one of whom was best friends of Farid's mother. This particular cousin had also decided to spend the weekend by the seaside and had summarily dragged an unwilling Sami down to Brighton. By the end of lunch a palpable frisson of interest was discerned. It was a veritable 'coup de foudre.' The next day a stunned Farid drove the newly hatched couple back to London, Jeffrey was contacted and various odd friends came around to ogle the sight of Beatrice in love. Jeffrey was around in a jiffy, accepted the unexpected union without question and diplomatically requested Sami's permission to take Beatrice to the Ugandan Embassy that very evening. As usual Jeffrey and Beatrice bonded over the anticipation of another interesting evening. President Amin was in town and there was a reception in his honour at the Embassy. Earlier in the year Jeffrey had accompanied the body of King Freddy, who had died penniless in London, back to Uganda for a State Funeral. Jeffrey, who had always claimed emphatically "I will never leave England until I have visited every nook and cranny," soon recanted when this offer had come up to join the official entourage. His cousin had been envious of the riveting account of the trip: so many toasts at the banquets that there was no time to eat, the safaris, his interesting comrades. All had participated in the theatre of this hypocritical show of homage. In fact, Amin had been involved in the downfall of King Freddie. Now Beatrice's hand was being crushed in Amin's vigorous handshake whilst Jeffrey cavorted amongst an admiring crowd of embassy officials. One leaned over and whispered in her ear, "If we had known Jeffrey had such a pretty cousin we would have included you in the trip to Uganda."

Plans for Europe were kept. Sami joined Beatrice and her group of friends traveling in an old rusty Volkswagen, crossing The English Channel by car ferry, passing through Brussels for afternoon tea with a friend originally from Liverpool. Helen was delighted to entertain the motley crew of people arriving unannounced on her doorstep. Then, onto their final destination: Amsterdam. The invitation originally had been offered only to Beatrice. When Samantha, heavily pregnant with a second child, saw the number of unexpected guests a hasty plan was conceived. Her son attended a kindergarten on the ground floor of an old house overlooking one of the canals. An emergency meeting with the children was held. They voted unanimously that the foreigners could stay on the upper floors of their school and even allow them access to their garden. And so, a temporary commune was born. After two weeks it was time for Beatrice and Sami to return to England, this time by train and ferry. The relationship between Beatrice and Sami had strengthened.

They made the trip up North. Her family was horrified to hear that she was off to the States and with such a disheveled looking young man of unknown provenance! Beatrice was compelled to reassure them that it was only for a few months.

As her new life began in New York, Jeffrey's royal encounters and social events increased at a dizzying rate.

For the first time it was necessary to actually write letters to keep in touch. Transatlantic phone calls were beyond their financial means.

A quarter of a century had passed by since her encounter with Sami and their journey through life together when Jeffrey died. His letters to Beatrice had miraculously survived. Through the vicissitudes of an arduous life, she had managed to save them all. And now that he was gone she felt compelled to go through them and perpetuate his memory.

The Letters: 1972-1974

J effreys' letters started not long after Beatrices' departure to New York. They were full of his colourful exploits and updates on their mutual friends and family. They muted the acute homesickness that Beatrice underwent. She missed the common bond of shared experience and the richness of phrase and vocabulary with which one joked and chatted. She missed cheshire and caerphilly cheese and steak and kidney pies and puddings with custard and a good cup of tea. She yearned for the rambles at weekends over the Welsh mountains or Sussex Downs with the patter of rain bathing one's face, inhaling the fresh smell of damp earth. But above all she missed Jeffrey, his wit and wicked sense of humour and yes, even his total self-absorption when delving into his beloved royals.

—∞—

1.X1.71.
116 Beaufort Street Chelsea

"Dear Beatrice,

I have been leading a particularly busy social life this last month, with more to come. I went down to Brighton for

Ramon and Jackie's wedding which was really lovely. Jackie wore a long cream dress with a pattern around the bottom and round the sleeves and she looked really sweet. Ramon was in a green velvet suit. It was the most wonderful October day —so warm it seemed like the middle of the summer, and we were able to have the reception in the garden. Everyone had more than enough champagne (in fact I hardly remember anything about the journey back home with Jackie's mum on the Brighton Belle). In all there were about 30 people and their garden provided an elegant setting for a most elegant gathering – as the late afternoon sun dipped over the folds of Brighton and turned from yellow to red, it was like the closing scene of a long and wonderful summer.

Last week I went to a party given by Princess Safia of Afghanistan in honour of Princess Elizabeth of Yugoslavia who is going to live in New York for a year. There were great mounds of Afghan food - steaming rice with meat embedded in it, etc. Also there was Sheikha Samiyat of Abu Dhabi, daughter of the ruler of Abu Dhabi. Tomorrow I'm going to the Red Cross Ball at Grosvenor House with Princess Safia, as part of her party.

I've had an invitation from Princess Dina of Jordan to attend her winter fashion show at the Dorchester next week, which should be quite fun, and the end of the month I'm going to the premier of "Nicolas and Alexandra." I've also been invited to what will be the first tea dance (thé dansant) to be held in London since the War. It is being given at the Café Royal by Lady Aylwen (you remember her from the Sealed Knott?).

I had a bit of fun last Friday when I tried my hand at entertaining Royalty for the first time. I took Prince Ali Vassib of Turkey out to Parsons for a meal. He was really turned on by all the potted palms and the atmosphere and also by the music. He's nearly 70 and all those palms must have given him a nostalgie d'enfance.

The State visit of the Emperor and Empress of Japan was most exciting, and made up in part for my not being able to go to Persepolis. I was hoping to get a phone call from Princess Anne to say she's bringing back a couple of cold peacock sandwiches!

I went to Count Tolstoy's wedding a couple of weeks ago at the Russian Church. It was a spectacular ceremony with the Russian Crowns being held over the heads of the bride and groom. As Nikolai is so tall the bishop accidentally let go of the crown and it dropped onto his head and he stood there for a couple of moments looking like a middle –European Grand Duke until one of the grooms stretched up to retrieve the crown.

Any idea when you'll be coming back? Looking forward to hearing from you, and my very best wishes to Sami.

Love Jeffrey

Updates on the Beacon family were also included. Beatrice sighed deeply, surveying her own situation so far away geographically and socially. They had been living close to Woodstock up in the hills on the estate of a famous folk singer. Sami was trying to come to terms with a deviated pathway, knocked off course by the politics of the 60's. Beatrice had taken the opportunity to find a position amongst the undisciplined entourage of a drugged-out performer. He was a southern gentleman and took a liking to his English 'housekeeper.' Apart from the hoards of musicians who dropped by or stayed for unplanned visits, her daily companions were a pack of dogs, just as unruly as the owner: Joseph, the magnificent patriarch, a huge fearsome looking Siberian husky and his mate Misha, also an imposing Siberian husky but not so fearful looking, their six puppies and a stray mutt. They made a marked contrast to Jeffrey's colourful life. Sami was away in New York City most of the time to work on different scenarios for their future whilst Beatrice's days were busy rescuing the dogs from all sorts of mishaps and cooking on a shoestring for the visitors.

When this first letter was received they had just returned back to the city. Living in the country would not be tenable now that the cold weather had set in. With their future uncertain she immersed herself in his news recalling the time when she had met Lady Alwyn and Count Tolstoy. The occasion was a celebratory drinking party made up of the Cavaliers who had just gloriously beaten the Roundheads in the reenactment of the battle fought during England's Civil War 1642-1651. Flushed with the exhilaration of victory the straggling group of spectators and participants gathered at an ancient pub somewhere in London. Beatrice tried hard to remember the name and location but these facts had already faded from her mind. The members of the society known as The Sealed Knot arrayed themselves at rickety tables on a wooden balcony, which projected over a cobbled courtyard, drinking gin and tonic. It was not hard to imagine a bygone era of horses and carts and maelstrom. Jeffrey had been in his element, bowing courteously and paying court to the various titled guests with a confident familiarity. Count Tolstoy was impressively handsome and worldly sophisticated. He was quite content to talk to Beatrice about his work, which at the time was teaching in grammar school. Lady Alwyn on the other hand sat rigidly on her hard backed chair extending her hand for receiving Jeffreys' gallant kiss but did not acknowledge the presence of anyone let alone Beatrice.

23.XII.71
116, Beaufort Street
Chelsea
S.W.3

"Dear Beatrice,

Thanks for your letter. I thought I would write before
Christmas as I set off to Brighton tomorrow with a couple
of ounces of fudge and a happy heart that a year well-
achieved is now nearly ended. I hope to see Ramon and
Jackie and I shall give them your love.

Remember Chris Jones? And how he always used to
appear at significant moments? Well, he did it again last
week. A Mass to celebrate the third anniversary of "Hair"
was held at St. Paul's Cathedral a couple of weeks ago.
I arrived to find that the cathedral was full and that
anyway you needed tickets to get in! Outside were about
1000 people, many demonstrating against the service,
but many also trying to get in. I managed, after about
fifteen minutes to push my way up the steps, but my way
was further blocked by about six policemen. So I stood at
the great door of the cathedral wondering how ever I was
going to get in when a voice behind called out my name.
It was Chris, clutching four tickets and trying like mad to
get through the crush. I just followed him and his party.
No sooner had I got through the door than it slammed shut
behind me, and after that no else got in! The service was
most impressive, with the entire cast of "Hair" singing hit
numbers from the show. Then communion was served to a
special Mass composed by Galt Macdermot. All the clergy
were in special vestments. I had a seat with Chris and his
party in a special section enclosure for "super- trendies",
up near the altar. If one considers the Piscean Age to be
typified by the advent of Christianity (and remember the

fish was a symbol of both!) and that after 2000 years both the Church and the Piscean Age seem to be ending, and that the Aquarian Age typified by the ideals of "Hair" is just beginning, then this service was like handing over the reins of power. It was indeed highly symbolic and I don't think that the clergy really understood what they were into.

My social life is "going a treat" still. We had a State visit a fortnight ago, of the King of Afghanistan and his daughter. I have visited the ex Queen Dina of Jordan, who is most charming, and last Sunday while looking round the Cecil Beaton Fashion Anthology at the Victorian and Albert Museum I chanced to turn around and find Queen Dina standing behind me.

When you get back we must have tea together at the Ritz Palm Court. It has to be seen to be believed. I go there fairly often, and as a contrast I go to the hard Rock Café on Piccadilly, which is like the G.A.D. but 10 times more so.

Any idea when you are coming back?

Crown Prince Alexander of Yugoslavia has announced his engagement to Princess Maria da Gloria of Brazil- the best dynastic marriage for years!

Looking forward to your news

Best wishes to Sami

Love
Jeffrey

7. 111. 72

Dear Beatrice,

Thanks very much for your letter.

It's strange you should have mentioned Diane in your letter. I bumped into her on the King's Road the day after I received your letter. I hadn't seen her for ages (except for a brief wave from a train on the other side of the platform of Sloane Square during New Year) She asked how you were and didn't seem to know what you were up to.

I met Christos at a party about a month ago – he is now married; in fact this was the day after the wedding. Also, there was Peter (I think that's the right name) –anyway, he was the boy who we ate a macrobiotic meal with at his flat once. Christos wanted to know what your news was and I told him you were engaged, and it seemed rather fitting that he too should be married.

The book is growing daily like a tropical jungle of exotic foliage. In the last week I've had a big breakthrough with the Yemen and Laos. Tomorrow I'm going to see a literary agent whose name I was given by a chance acquaintance. When I phoned, I learnt she'd already heard all about me from this acquaintance. Anyway, she seems very interested.

Have you any idea when you'll be coming to London?

I'm halfway through "Der Steppenwolf"- I don't know if I like it too much–it seems to counteract my joie de vivre by its pessimism and despondency.

You must go and see 'The Boyfriend'. It's very camp and funny and Twigs is marvelous. I went to see "A Clockwork Orange" – which I was going to have a part as an extra in, but then they cancelled the scene. Its very violent and not terribly brilliant. "The Devils" is good – I finally caught up with that a few weeks ago. But I still

think the best film of 1971 was "Death in Venice." I want
to see it again, but I keep missing it by a few days.

My best wishes to Sami
Lots of love and kisses
Jeffrey

Beatrice, in the meantime, had effortlessly acquired the much sought-after Green Card and had a proper job at Mt Sinai working as a pharmacist once more, not sure whether to be pleased or not.

Jeffrey's letter momentarily aroused an ire since it referred to two people she would have preferred to forget. Diane had been an older student at University and seemed to think that the girl from Liverpool knew the path to Nirvana. She relentlessly followed her from flat to flat, unwanted since she was oblivious to other peoples' needs, a sensitivity much needed in sharing rooms in flats. And when she heard that Beatrice was off to New York she stated she would come too. "If she ends up on the same flight I'm not going," she had told Sami. She turned up a week later staying with the father of an old boyfriend who was serving time in prison on a drug related offense. For some reason Beatrice and Sami accepted a dinner at the apartment of Diane's host in Brooklyn. It was shabby, dingy and untidy just like the owner who was a retired lawyer, divorced and who had the distinction of being the lawyer for The Living Theatre. As they embarked on desultory conversation, Diane suddenly perked up. "Now that you have found the love of your life," she announced dramatically, flourishing back her lanky hair, and staring at Sami, "I can tell you, that while you were with the theatre group in France," a malicious glance was thrown in her direction, "Christos and I ————." Beatrice glared at her with such venom that Diane had faltered, knowing full well not to continue. The table was silent. Sami understood immediately. When they left Beatrice vowed never to see her again. Christos had been the harrowing obsessional affair that had gone on the year before. Diane had followed Beatrice from a Pimblico residence to Oakley Street, weaseling her way into this flat even though Beatrice had forewarned the other girl there not to take her on. And so, Diane had seen first-hand how Beatrice had suffered at the hands of this charismatic but thoroughly unsuitable suitor.

As for Christos, an older Greek architect, who once stated to her that "the only person he would tolerate on a daily basis was his friend Peter," had been horrified that she was leaving England. Their relationship had ended six months earlier, by Beatrice who had finally come to her senses. So she had never understood how he could have known she was in London, on the eve of her departure with Sami. He had come by unexpected to Oakley Street and taking her out of earshot of Sami told her: "You are making a big mistake going to America. Come with me to Greece. I will introduce you to my mother who I know will like you very much." She had laughed gaily at this absurd offer. Sami had bravely waited in the lounge thinking that their whirlwind romance was over.

Now all had been made clear.

4.IV.72

Dear Beatrice,

Thanks very much for your letter. Sorry I wasn't more explicit, but there's not a lot I can say.

Christos's wife is neither a virginal Greek nor a wealthy vamp. She is English, fairly dark, and to be quite honest I can't remember any more about her as I was stoned at the time and my attention was attracted to other matters. But it was rather a coincidence meeting him the day after his wedding!

I'm glad to hear you've been able to get a job. Is it interesting?

I've just got back from Brighton. I saw Ramon and Jackie but they left on the second day I was there for a holiday in Spain. I also saw toutes les Nonoos, and they were all very interested to hear your news and plans, but

I couldn't tell them very much. I understand from Mrs. Nonoo (Farid's mother) that Sami's sister is now married, following the commotion you described so vividly in your letter.

I came back on the Brighton Belle yesterday —in three weeks time it is to make its last run and I have tickets for this. It includes champagne the journey down, dinner in the banqueting hall of the Brighton Pavilion and a special farewell ceremony at Brighton Station where a military band and choir will perform the "Railroad Song" by Hector Berlioz. The departure of the Belle from Brighton will then be accompanied by a gigantic fireworks display. This is all organized as part of the Brighton Festival.

I heard via Liverpool that you nearly came home for a week at Easter. If you come between now and July as you say in your letter, will you be coming for just a week or longer? Everyone in Brighton is longing to see you.

Next week is a big Royal week for me- the State Visit of Queen Juliana and Prince Bernhard of the Netherlands. This is the third Royal State visit in six months - first we had the Emperor and Empress of Japan, then the King and Princess Bilquis of Afghanistan. Usually there is some wretched president in between the Royal ones, but now it is three in a row.

Looking forward to hearing from you soon,

Lots of love
Jeffrey
Xxx

—◈—

Beatrice planned a visit to England, overcome by acute homesickness. There she introduced Sami to her greatest passion, horse riding. Seeing the sheer happiness illuminating his face after an exhilarating gallop it was understood they would be sharing this pastime together.

On their way back to the States, traveling from Liverpool, Jeffrey spent the last evening with them in London. They tearfully embraced at the bottom of a steep bank of escalators in the Tube. Jeffrey walked off in one direction as they ascended to street level and there was Jeffrey! They all laughed hysterically, tears of merriment adorning their cheeks. It was a magical and memorable send off.

—ɷ—

1ˢᵗ June 1972

Dear Beatrice,

Many thanks for your letter. I'm glad you saw about the Brighton Belle in 'Time.' The last journey was one of the most enjoyable events I've ever been on. We left Victoria at 7pm in brilliant sunshine, and on the journey each passenger consumed half a bottle of champagne (on an empty stomach). We were handed carnations, cigarettes, cigars, little bottles of whisky and photographs of the Belle – incidentally as we left Victoria a quartet of musicians played music by the Prince Regent. On arrival in Brighton there was a great crowd at the station and we were led like Royalty through it by the police, to awaiting coaches, which then took us to the Royal Pavilion. I have never seen the Palace look so marvelous – with all the curtains drawn the rooms assumed their original splendour. There were palms and ferns everywhere, specially put there for the occasion. Firstly, we had drinks in the Music Room, then walked through for dinner in the Banqueting Room. The meal was extremely good and was accompanied by a genuine palm court orchestra of doddery men. After the sweet we were served with Canapes Brighton Belle, which turned out to be kippers on toast – in honour of the famous Brighton Belle kippers, which Lord Olivier immortalized in 1968 when he led a campaign against British Railways who wanted to remove them from the Belle menu. He won.

As these festivities occurred on the 80th birthday of Empress Zita of Austria I decided to ask the Mayor – at the top table –whether, as we were in a Royal Palace, we could toast Her Imperial Majesty, who is the last European Empress. I went up to the top table, and he agreed it would be nice to toast her, but unfortunately his advisor said not to as the Press might get the wrong idea.

After the meal we assembled on the balcony of the Pavilion and there was the fireworks display on the lawns, the finale of which was a model of the Brighton Belle which moved across the lawn. We were bundled back onto the coaches and taken to the Station for the grand climax of the evening– a never to be repeated performance of the "Railroad Song" by Hector Berlioz, performed by the massed band of the Coldstream Guards (about 60 musicians) and the Concordia Choir of Crawley (120 voices in all). They were already assembled on the platform when we arrived, and then they began to play the incredible "Railroad Song"– a Victorian oration of the power of steam – which continued for six verses and choruses. There was hardly a dry eye in the station. When they had finished a group of passengers began singing "Rule Britannia", and the choir decided, quite spontaneously, to join in. This too went on for several choruses and verses, until finally we all boarded the train, and a trumpeter leaned out of the window of the last carriage and played the Reveille as the Belle moved out of Brighton Station for the very last time. By chance I had been pushed into the carriage with the trumpeter and had the curious sight of seeing the station platform gradually disappear while the silhouette of a trumpet floated in front of me. When I returned to my carriage the man opposite was singing a famous love song called (I think) "Aloa-aho" written by the last queen of Hawaii, Queen Liliuokalani, and which I have never heard sung in public before! On the return journey we were served with more champagne and cucumber sandwiches. The whole evening was just like the Shah's Persopolis celebrations, with one treat leading to another.

On Saturday I am going down to Windsor for the lying-in- state of the Duke of Windsor. On Monday is the funeral and I shall be going to that also, although it is supposed to be private. There have been great manifestations of sympathy in London, and I was surprised such a fuss should be made. There has been nothing in the Press other than accounts of the Dukes' life since he died four days ago. The great State Bell at St. Paul's Cathedral was tolled for an hour on Tuesday- it was last rung on the death of King George V1 in 1952! It weighs 17 and ½ tons and takes four men to ring it — the sound was like from another world — in fact it poured with rain, and it was as if it was the end of the world as the great booms rang out across the city.

I spent the Bank Holiday in Brighton – it was unbelievably cold, wet and windy, and with the news of the Dukes' death in the middle of the weekend, it wasn't much fun (all flags and bunting were removed from the Palace Pier and a Union Jack flew at half-mast over the dodgems on the Promenade). I saw Ramon and Jackie, and Farid, and spent a bizarre hour in Ramon's mothers' fantasy parlour, during which I was shown, amongst other weird and amazing things, a bucket of mushrooms growing in the lavatory at the end of the garden! Do you remember the wallpaper in the room (not the leopard skin wallpaper – the other one which consists of great golden bows and knots); well, she told me not to touch it in case the knots came undone and the room fell down – and I believed her!

June and July are to be extremely busy- after the State Funeral there is to be a the first and last ever Grand Ducal State Visit to London – the Grand Duke and Grand Duchess of Luxembourg are to be here for three days. Then the next week there is the Knights of the Garter Ceremony at Windsor, for which I have a ticket, and this year Emperor Haile Selassie (80) is to be installed as a Knight of the Garter- the thought of a Reigning Emperor in Garter freaks me out. Then there is Royal Ascot for four days. Then the official engagement of Crown Prince Alexander of Yugoslavia to Princess Maria da Gloria of Brazil, in the Serbian Church "in a remote corner of Bayswater" (quote from Oscar Wilde's "The Importance of Being Ernest" – see Lady Bracknell's speech in the last act). On 1ˢᵗ July I fly out to Seville for the actual wedding ceremony, which could be described as intercontinental dynastic. The bride numbers amongst her uncles and aunts the Pretenders to the Thrones of France, Spain and Portugal, and another aunt was born a Princess of Egypt. The following week is the wedding of Prince Richard of Gloucester in England, and two weeks after that the French Royal Wedding in Normandy. In August I shall probably have to take the cure at Baden-Baden to recover!

It was really super seeing you and Anwar in London and our trip to the Hard Rock was great fun. I hope I didn't startle you too much by appearing behind you on the escalator.

I could go on forever, but I must stop now as there is much to be done.

Very best wishes to Sami

Lots of love
Jeffrey xxx

A postcard from Seville dated July 1972:-

Dear Beatrice and Sami,

I'm in Seville for the Brazilian/Yugoslav Royal wedding. I'm staying at the Alfonso X111 Hotel. It's filthy with Royalty. I'm beginning to lose count how many there are. Princess Ann is staying here as well.

Love Jeffrey

P.S. Just seen Duchess Barbara of Mecklenberg

116 Beaufort Street
24. V11. 72.

Dear Beatrice,

Thanks very much for your letter and especially for the picture, which I was very pleased to receive. I have not got it in my collection; in fact I have never seen it before, and it will find a welcome place in my album of portraits of the Royal House of Stuart.
I hope you have recovered from the 'flu by now.
Do you know, is just five years since I made my very first visit to Chelsea, and I came to see you in Oakley Street. You were in a flat near the King's Road end at the time —remember? And you had a friend called Mike who wrote poetry. We met Sonia for a drink at the Chelsea Potter.
The wedding of the Crown Prince of Yugoslavia and Princess Maria da Gloria of Brazil was absolutely fantastic. It took place in the garden of Prince Pedro of

Brazil's Palace about 20 miles outside Seville, at twilight.
There were about 70 Royal Highnesses present! The
guest of honour was of course Princess Anne. The several
hundred other guests included high Spanish and Portugese
aristocrats, Yugoslav and Brazilian Monarchists, jet-set
friends of Princess Maria da Gloria, hippie friends of her
long haired brothers, British army officer friends of Crown
Prince Alexander (he was in the army until his marriage
and in fact served in Northern Ireland), and all sorts of
people like myself who had just turned up for the fun of it.
I was amazed to find three people near me were handing
round a joint in the middle of the ceremony! No —one could
smell it as the priests' incense and the scents of the flowers
in the garden overpowered it. I was dying for a drag but
couldn't bring myself to ask them.

After the service there was a reception in the Palace
courtyard, which is in the centre of the building; in the
centre was a massive palm tree. Then after the reception
the gates at the far end were thrown open and outside was
a fountain, behind which was another garden, surrounded
by palm trees, with tables laid for 800. We went through
for dinner, following which there was a display of flamenco
dancing. To give you an idea of the exotic Royals present
her is a selection of some of them:-

Her Imperial and Royal Highness the Archduchess
Robert of Austria-Este.

Their Royal Highness the Count and Countess of
Paris (King and Queen of France).

His Royal Highness the Infante Alsonso of Spain (aged
85- grandson in-law of Queen Victoria and great-great-
uncle of the bridegroom).

His Majesty King Umberto of Italy.

Their Majesty King Constantine and Queen Ann-
Marie of Greece.

Their Royal Highness Prince Juan Carlos and Princess Sofia of Spain (Franco's heirs).

His Royal Highness Prince Francisco of Brazil. Her Imperial and Royal Highness Grand Duchess Valeria of Baden (niece of Prince Philip by marriage)

Her Royal Highness Princess Ana of the Two Sicilies.

His Royal Highness the Crown Prince of of Portugal.

His Royal Highness Prince Paul, ex-Prince regent of Yugoslavia.

Her Royal Highness Princess Ann.

Etc

I was mistaken for a cousin of the bride, Count Zamoyaki, by the brides' father, and put into the procession of Royal guests; later the bride's aunt Princess Teresa of Brazil started speaking to me in Portugese, also thinking I was the Count, and when I said I wasn't she said but you look just like him- the hair, the velvet suit. Then the Infanta Pilar of Spain also thought I was him. And later still, I was mistaken for Princess Ann's hairdresser by the British Ambassador! The hotel was incredible- rather like the one in "Death in Venice"- there was Royalty everywhere; in the lifts, on the stairs, in the hall and the dining room, even one morning, outside my bedroom, where the children of the King of Greece and the Prince of Spain were playing when I opened my door. I was stopped on the stairs one evening by the Archduchess Rosemary of Austria who asked if I'd seen the King of Italy. It was like a fantasy world – imagine being asked where the King of Italy was on a No.14 bus! Especially by the Archduchess of Austria!

At the wedding one woman was wearing the Order of the Rose of Brazil, last bestowed on anybody in 1889!

The night after the wedding I went to another party at the Palace, this time for the Brazilians who had come over for the wedding. All the Brazilian Imperial Family were present and most of the French Royal Family (the Countess of Paris was born a Princess of Brazil).

Well, I could go on forever, but I think by now you must have some idea of the hothouse atmosphere of the occasion.

I hear you'll be in England in the not too distant future. Please let me know when. Looking forward to hearing from you.

Best wishes to Sami

Love,
Jeffrey

Meanwhile back in the States the tempestuous relationship between Beatrice and Sami endured the complex cultural differences between them. A decision was made to visit England in August. Neither of them was interested in a formal marriage. In contrast to Jeffrey's wedding invites, there was no merging of great dynasties, no dowry to consider. After heated discussions: "but you know my parents won't let us sleep together", "but I faint with blood tests!" (Sami referred to the syphilis test required at the time for a marriage license) "Oh don't be ridiculous" scoffed Beatrice. She had great compassion for her mother. After all, her daughter had run off to New York professing she lived with Sami's sister, although she knew better, and how long could they live together while her mother feigned holding up her proud Beacon head? A compromise was reached. A rabbi was found who after initial reservations accepted to do the deed. He had been concerned since neither of the couple wanted any family present at the ceremony. However, Sami had presented such a well thought out explanation that the rabbi conceded but requested four witnesses: two of Sami's uncles, his sister and brother-in-law. A friend from work, Arthur, was added to the guest list.

Beatrice had called home. "I have good news Mum." At the end of the line the excitement was palpable. Her mother was preparing to hear news of a formal engagement, which would then be circulated throughout the clan before the day was over. "We have just got married." Silence. The magnitude of her mother's disappointment said it all.

The next day they landed in London and made their way up North.

But timing is all. The Finestones had just moved into yet another home. The bungalow without a front door had been abandoned and now Aunt Freda's dream of viewing the sea had been fulfilled. They had acquired a home in Lythm St.Annes where the living room was on the upper floor permitting a sweeping panorama of seascape. A huge party was in the making the very next day.

Having carefully scrutinized the Katuba (wedding contract) in the driveway of her home they were accepted as the new Mr. and Mrs. S. and welcomed with open arms by a relieved father. No mortgage was needed to celebrate this event. And furthermore, the family was being assembled in its entirety the next day thanks to the Finestones! Her father was ecstatic. "You have saved me a lot of money," he whispered in her ear. Her mother was still concerned, wondering what all the relatives would say.

The guests arrived in dribs and drabs. Climbing up from the ground floor, which accommodated the kitchen and bedrooms, one reached the upper level opening up into a huge, high ceilinged living room with vast picture windows looking out on a dazzling view of the shimmering Irish Sea. Once all the guests had gathered together an announcement was made and the atmosphere shifted from a house warming to a wedding celebration. Beatrice and Sami beamed victoriously. "Not bad eh?" said Sami. All the Beacons, the huge extended family on Beatrice's mother's side who had all conveniently settled in the Liverpool area, were present. Jeffrey had journeyed up from London. Robert was up from Cambridge University huddled in a corner with his younger cousin Carolyn (half sister of Robin). After imbibing a few drinks, a disorderly line of guests meandered its way to the luncheon held at a nearby hotel. Robert, in a fit of rebelliousness, refused to participate in such a bourgeois event. On the way back, walking along the Promenade, Jeffrey grumbled at his parents' parsimonious ways, having noted that the champagne was not up to quality and that he was for sure going to suffer from a headache.

Guests lingered on viewing the setting sun and watching the evening clouds gather as night fell. Being seasonably warm the windows were flung open and some guests descended downstairs spilling out into the garden, drinks in hand, savouring the sea breeze and recounting much loved family tales. Sami was a huge success and even Beatrice's mother was satisfied when her brother-in-law Karl, the acknowledged intellect and historian in the family, spoke well of him.

Journeying down south, Beatrice and Sami and Jeffrey met up with Jackie and Ramon and hung out in the notorious store of Ramon's mother. Behind the stacks of porn magazines, a very short lady with her beehive-peroxided hair was barely visible behind the shop counter. She entertained them all with tea and cakes in her parlour with the gaudy wallpaper and they delighted in her raucous stories related with a strong cockney accent and a cackling laugh.

5th Sept. 1972
116 Beaufort Street
(sent to Beatrice's home in Liverpool)

Dear Beatrice and Sami,

It was lovely seeing you on Sunday and I hope you enjoyed yourselves as much as I did.

I'm just writing a short note to say I'll be around on Saturday and it would be super if we all went to tea at the Ritz (as I vaguely remember arranging something about it with you late on Sunday night!). However, ring me at my office some time between now and Friday to finalize it. Robert wants to see you both, but won't want to come to the Ritz. So we can meet up on Sunday in Clapton or something.

I've got the photos of you in Brighton and they're nearly as good as yours.

Robert and I broke off our journey back yesterday to have a look at the Preston Guild – how's this for kitchness: plastic Union Jacks!!

Lots of love
Jeffrey

P.S. There's one problem with the Ritz; you have to wear a tie. Sami, you can borrow one of mine if you're short. However if Paris was worth a mass to Henry 1V then the Ritz is worth a tie any day.

—ᴍᴍ—

27ᵗʰ September 1972
116 Beaufort Street

Dear Beatrice and Sami,

It was super seeing you while you were here, and especially pleasant seeing you against the happy background of Brighton at Bank Holiday and the party in Lytham. Here are the pictures I took in Brighton – I shall send the ones I took of the party later, when I've had some more copies made. Please let me have some of the ones you took in Brighton, as I very much want to put them in my album.

At the end of this week I begin working full time for Burke's and shall be technically self-employed: which means I will not have to keep office hours and other such shit. I'm hoping life will become one endless spree.

I thought you would like to read this very interesting article from 'Time Out,' which mentions Treteaux Libres.

I'm off to Portugal in a fortnight for the Spanish Royal wedding, and shall let you know how I get on. Next week is Richard Smith's wedding, at Claridges, and I shall send you an (albeit amusing) account of that as well. (Did you hear about the Jewish lady who thought that R.S.V.P. on the bottom of an invitation meant "remember send vedding present"?)

I spent the weekend at Windsor with Mummy and Daddy. The Windsor Festival was on and we heard Menuhin and Ashkenazy play. On one day we went on a Victorian Society walk around the town and the Castle, and saw amongst other things, the Royal Waiting Room at the railway station. The woman who showed us around kept reading quotes from Queen Victorias' diaries, and I had a hard job keeping a straight face when she read out the following passage about Prince Albert's home in Germany "And I saw the little bedroom where dear Albert and his brother used to sleep with the tutor!"

I think it was the way the woman read it out that gave it the double entendre — but it was a very dull crowd and no-one else seemed to get it.

Well, I think that's all my news for now.

Write soon,
Lots of love,
Jeffrey

The cutting from 'Time Out' brought Beatrice back to the time not long after she had left the theatre group. It was early 1971.

Treteaux had been brought over to London to perform at the Young Vic Theatre. Beatrice had journeyed down to London, staying with Christos, to see the group in the new production "Fusion", which she had helped create. They went together to the performance. Seating was arranged in a circular fashion with the performing space in the centre. Startling to see was that across from them was Jeffrey sitting next to Ley! They looked especially comfortable and intimate together.

She tried to remember what they had done afterwards to no avail. The encounter with the members of the group was deeply emotional and distressing since Bernard the director was trying to seduce her back to join them again.

———⟪⟫———

12ᵗʰ December 1972
116 Beaufort Street

Dear Beatrice and Sami,

Many thanks for your letter of 20ᵗʰ October and for the wonderful photographs. I'm sorry I haven't replied sooner, but I have been madly busy.

The trip to Portugal was wonderful. The Crown Prince of Portugal excelled himself by not only arranging for me to go to the party at the Spanish Pretender's villa, but he actually called for me at my hotel in his car and drove me there. I was quite amazed when the phone went and he announced himself, saying he was in the entrance of the hotel! The party was marvelous and there was ample opportunity to speak to whichever Royal I wished. As it happened a lot of them recognized me. The wedding, the following day, was simpler than the other two I went to, but a very happy family occasion. As you know the Infanta Margarita of Spain is blind, and so the occasion was really very unusual. Among the guests were nearly all the Spanish Royal Family, including Prince Juan Carlos and Princess Sofia as well as King Umberto of Italy, King Duarte of Portugal and his three sons, fourteen members of the Royal family of the Two Sicilies (the bride's mother was a born princess of that family), Princess Teresa and Princess Pia of Brazil, the Duke of Bourbon-Parma and the Countess of Paris and her daughter Princess Chantel (whose wedding I went to in July). The wedding lunch was held at the hotel I was staying at and I was to photograph everyone at the tables and in the reception.

I spent the rest of the holiday visiting Royals in their houses, and I was made very welcome by everybody. I started off with King Umberto of Italy, who I had to see about a booklet, which some people in England want to write about him. The next day I went for morning drinks to Princess Teresa of Brazil's house and she invited her sister the Countess of Paris and Princess Chantal to come, as I told her I would be bringing my photos of the last two Royal weddings. Between them they ordered over sixty photographs (from the album you looked at in Lytham), which they insisted on paying for. It was quite an honour sitting on the sofa next to the rightful Queen of France while she chose and commented on pictures of her daughters' wedding.

The most interesting part of the visit was my trip to Lisbon one evening when I was the guest of the Crown Prince. He took me to dinner in a fantastic restaurant, deep in the old Arab quarter of the city. It looked like a private house at the end of a very dark alley, and inside it was like a family kitchen. The food was out of this world. We started with gigantic slices of melon, followed by some strange cooked sausage, then the largest trout I've ever eaten, then steak and finally grapes served with ice. The proprietor made a great fuss of us and kept addressing the

Crown Prince as "Altessa." Between courses he played the guitar. Then I was taken on a conducted tour of the city; it was my first visit and the Crown Prince proved an excellent guide- after all it is his capital city.

On the last night in Portugal I went inside Lisbon again for an exhibition of paintings by Princess Ikbal of Egypt. King Umberto, realizing I was interested in non–European Royalty, had got me an invitation for it. Princess Ikbal was very surprised to see me as we had last met at her brothers' house in London.

Since I've been back I've followed the Silver Wedding very closely. One night I spent the evening in the lounge at Claridges watching the foreign royals come and go. The actual celebrations were a great success and the Queen and Prince Philip are more popular than ever.

I went to see "Sauvage Messiah" last week, but didn't enjoy it as much as other Ken Russell films. Also I saw "Jesus Christ Superstar", which was rather heavy. I thought it would be more joyous like "Hair".

I went home for the weekend a couple of weeks ago, and came back to London via Liverpool where I visited Aunty Baile. She is now home and a lot better. I hadn't seen her for nearly three years and felt I really had to make the effort. I found that same wavelength we always used to share was still there. I think she is the most 'aware' member of our family.

I'm enclosing a leaflet about the book I've just finished working on. It comes out in February. Burke's want me to help with the research on a book, which is to show all descendants of American presidents. I've agreed to do it although I'm not very excited about the idea. However, when this is finished they'll probably publish my book on the Royal Families of the world, so I have to go ahead with it. Of course, when the American book is published I should

*think I'd go with it and the author on a promotional tour
in the States.*

*Well, I don't think this letter and card will arrive in time
for Christmas now, but all the best for the New Year,*

*Lots of love
Jeffrey*

As Beatrice read through this letter she understood that despite his entrée into the titled families of Europe, her cousin never lost sight of his roots in Liverpool. "He simply adores Aunt Baile," she reported to Sami, "You know, the Aunt who used take him around the auction houses at a young age. Don't you think she has that aura of bohéme?" Sami agreed that, in the brief time he had met her at their impromptu wedding reception, she certainly exhibited a 'knowing look' and appeared to be brimming with stories to tell.

1974-1980

7

By September of 1973 Sami and Beatrice had given up their studio on Madison Ave at 84th Street, as charming as it was with the sloping skylight and access to the rooftop. Now they had a more spacious apartment in Washington Heights. Decisions had finally been made, if not with trepidation. Sami returned to school to study the Basic Sciences at City College. He had decided to become a Veterinarian, in fact even more specifically, a Horse Vet. As for Beatrice it appeared Sami wanted all her dreams fulfilled. Whilst he studied the sciences she was to take up Art for which purpose she also enrolled at City College for Life Drawing, Design and Water Colour. In return she was to be his study partner the following year when she would attend Medical School, along with Sami at the Veterinarian School, in Bologna Italy. It all sounded too good to be true. Back to Europe and to Italy no less! The year flew by: art projects to complete, helping Sami with chemistry and physics, forms to send off to the Italian Consulates in New York and London, Saturday morning classes at the New School for immersion into the Italian Language, and horse riding as often as they could.

—∽—

Postcard sent May 18th 1974 from Monte Carlo:-

Dear Beatrice and Sami,

*I'm in Monte Carlo for Prince Rainier's Silver Jubilee –
lots of fireworks and brass bands, etc.*
*Tomorrow I'm going to the Cannes Film festival as
Prince Tate of Albania's guest.*

Love,
Jeffrey

[Many years later when they met up in the States, Jeffrey reported that he had obtained an interview with Princess Grace, the famous American actress Grace Kelly who was married to Prince Rainier. "She did very well as a royal," he had explained with some admiration, "but she made one mistake a real royal would never make!" "And what was that?" He patiently and meticulously explained that throughout her audience with him she bore her title well, behaving impeccably. However, at the end of the interview she made the dreadful and revealing mistake of standing up and escorting him to the door to see him out. He was most disappointed that her 'commoner' background had got the better of her depriving him of the satisfaction of ritualistically backing out as he bowed to a royal presence.]

116 Beaufort Street
18th May 1974

Dear Beatrice and Sami,

*Many thanks for your card – delighted to hear you will be
passing through London at the beginning of June.*

Please excuse only a short note, but I have just got back from Monte Carlo and I am trying to catch up on all sorts of things.

Yes, I shall be around until 7ᵗʰ June – I have to go to St. Annes then as Princess Ann is attending a concert on the Pier to mark the centenary of the town.

The Jubilee was fantastic – will tell you about it when I see you. I hope you got my card.

Safe journey

Lots of love
Jeffrey

With the blessing of Sami's father, they set off via London in June 1974 to Italy overwhelmed by the sheer audacity of starting new careers in their late twenties in a foreign language. They stayed at the flat of Sami's cousin in North London when the weather was at its worst providing a penetrating damp atmosphere from incessant rain. The grey skies amplified their apprehension. One way or another they did not get to see Jeffrey.

After three glorious carefree months in Perugia, honing their skills in communication at the 'Università per Gli Stranieri', they moved into the basement of a villa in 'la zona verde' up in the hills outside Bologna. The estate belonged to a successful industrialist, Signore Barbiera. It was replete with wild peacocks, which would settle on the grounds at dusk, the males spreading their voluptuous plumage and strutting about emitting thrilling raucous calls. When there was a full moon this call of the wild lasted throughout the night. Signora Barbiera abhorred this cry of nature and so the family never stayed in their luxurious abode.

Their time there was enchanting. In autumn inebriating vapours from fermented grapes, kept in the cellar ready to be pressed for wine making, engulfed their senses. Over the winter when persistent fog assailed the plains below, they would drive back from a city covered by impenetrable clouds, heavy with dankness and doom, and at a certain point emerge to a sun filled vista. One memorable night they had driven back from the city obscured by yet another fog. Emerging from the car they were bathed in an unearthly brightness. The brim of the veranda of the terrace, which overlooked a deep valley, was level with the topmost layer of dense cloud. Like a spotlight, a full moon shone down illuminating a frothy sea of fantastical shifting shapes.

It was a period of political unrest and kidnappings in Italy. When the son of their nearest neighbour, the Segrafredo's, was kidnapped they acquired a dog fearful they would be mistaken for the owners of the estate. He was named Circo.

Planning to start a family, they then found more suitable quarters in a village outside of Bologna called Ozzano dell'Emilia, moving there the following summer of 1975.

Jeffrey had also changed his address:-

27, Cheyne Walk,
London, S.W.3.
24th January, 1975

Dear Beatrice,

Many thanks for your letter – it was lovely hearing from you again.

I think you and Sami are very enterprising choosing to live in Italy and study there.

Many thanks indeed for the picture of Prince Umberto (later King Umberto 1), which I was very pleased to receive. It was very kind of you to think of getting it for me.

I wish you could see my new flat - it was ironic that you should have been so close to it in July, but had been unable to visit it. Now it is looking really good and the view of the Thames is even better in the winter as the leaves have fallen from the tree in front of the house to reveal a complete panorama.

Two weeks ago I traveled to Germany for a Royal wedding — Princess Elisabeth of Schleswig-Holstein was married at the Royal Castle of Glücksburg, close to the Danish border. It was very picturesque- the wedding took place in the Castle Chapel and there were sixty-five Princes and Princesses present. The evening before there had been a ball at which tiaras and orders were worn, and there were some magnificent sets of jewels.

Next month I am going to Nepal for the Coronation of King Birendra. I shall stay in Kathmandu for a fortnight. Two days before I leave, there will be an influx of Beacons in to the capital - Uncle Arthur, Eva, Uncle Bill and Auntie Edna will be flying in from Bangkok on their far east Asian tour. My father's old rhyme still holds true ("Wherever you may roam, on land or sea or foam, O'er all the four points of the compass, You're sure to meet, a Beacon, a Bennett or a Clumpus!")

Life in London still keeps me incredibly busy and satisfied. Although I love traveling in my quest for new Royal information I still find London a marvelous city to live in.

I was sorry I didn't see you when you were last over, but I presume you didn't get to London. When will you be over next? We really must get together properly this time- for at least an afternoon, if not longer.

With all my love to you and Sami,
Jeffrey

—m—

Not long after moving to Ozzano, Beatrice became pregnant. It was a brutally hot summer and they drove off to England only to discover it was just as hot there. In fact the land was scorched. Together they paid a visit to Auntie Baile and Uncle Harry who now lived in Southport just outside Liverpool. Aunt Baile was very ill but did her best to welcome them. Sami drove back to Bologna leaving Beatrice to cope with the first trimester in the comfort of her parents home.

Aunt Baile died two weeks after Beatrice returned to Bologna. The promised stories were never revealed.

—⁓—

29th November 1975

Dear Beatrice,

I realize with horror that that I have not replied to your letter of 7th October.

I have been extremely busy recently. At the time it arrived I was in Spain for the wedding of the King and Queen of Albania, and when I got back I had lots to catch up on.

I was delighted to hear about your baby and send you and Sami my sincerest congratulations.

It was very sad about Aunty Baile. I was pleased to hear about your meeting with her this summer. I last saw her in April when she and Uncle Harry came over to St. Annes.

My book will finally be published in about a years' time and it is hoped that it will coincide with the Queen's Silver Jubilee.

Many thanks for the cutting about Lady Ursula d'Abo- very interesting.

Did you hear about the present that Juan Carlos wanted to give to Franco- a turtle. Franco said he was very sorry but couldn't accept it as he would be so upset when it died!

With all my love to you and Sami
Jeffrey

—ᗰ—

As Beatrice continued to review the letters she discovered that between November 1975 January 1979 there were none! Were they lost or were the events in those ensuing years just too traumatic for Jeffrey to write? Certainly Beatrice had been busy.

She had two children, both born in Bologna, her very demanding studies, a house to run and a deep concern that Sami was not going to finish his studies. A year after the birth of their daughter they had moved to the other side of Bologna next to a village called Riale. Her eldest, Daniela, was enrolled in the local 'asilo nido' and the youngest, Gabriele, had his own 'dada' (babysitter) who came each day to their home. They now lived in a 'casa colonica', a gentleman farmer's villa.

When they first moved in the summer of 1977, the gardener, aptly named Signor Alberi, had greeted them with an enormous straw basket of freshly picked cherries from the estate. An auspicious start to a period in her life Beatrice deeply cherished. As the summer wore on unsolicited sprays of water freshened the boxes of geraniums, which festooned the windows of a spacious kitchen. Of course it was Signor Alberi, outside with a huge watering can and impressively long spout. He took good care of the expanse of grounds, having been with the family, i Signori Bonvicini, for decades. At the back of the villa a terrace faced the grand park with an allée of trees lining a central pathway. This led to the family church at the bottom, now home to numerous black scorpions, all religious artifacts having long ago been stolen.

But that same year of beatitude for Beatrice had turned into a dreadful year of inquietude for Jeffrey.

The Silver Jubilee was commemorated on February 6th 1977. Beatrice had been scanning the British papers for a review on Jeffery's book.

It was through an announcement in The London Times that she read the review of Burke's "Royal Families of the World" in which excerpts were printed. Jeffrey's distinctive voice was clearly apparent. Horrified that there was no mention of her cousin being the author, she sent off a letter to the newspaper requesting an explanation. Their reply was apologetic. They had contacted Burke's Peerage without any success. Through her family she heard that Jeffrey had requested an injunction on publication. His solicitor, non other than Uncle Arthur, was at that time held up in the Panama Canal whilst on a cruise. There was a strike. Auntie Freda would not request her other brother Peter to intervene "he is a barrister and can't be disturbed." By the time Arthur returned it was too late. It was said that Jeffrey had broken a contract by writing for other Monarchy magazines. This empowered Burke's to snatch the glory. Jeffrey was devastated. It was a watershed of tragedy that marked the rest of Jeffrey's life. The book that he had worked on for so long with such joy and diligence was not published in his name nor were there any acknowledgements. He succumbed to illness and was nursed back to health by an 'aristocratic lady' somewhere in London, as reported by the family.

—⁂—

27 Cheyne Walk
10th January 1979

Dear Beatrice,

Many thanks for your card and letter. Was very pleased to hear about Gabriele - I heard his name from Liverpool and guessed you would be using the Italian spelling.

I thought of you the day your letter arrived as I took a friend to sign the visitors' book at Buckingham Palace and recalled the day we went to sign it in the summer of 1970. Gosh, how time flies!

I spent six exhilarating weeks in New York last summer and fell in love with it. At present I'm writing a biography of Prince Dimitri of Russia — he's 77 and a nephew of Emperor Nicholas 11. Work is going very well and I see him every other day. His memory is very good and he seems to have met just about everyone — Rasputin (whom his brother-in-law, Prince Felix Youssanoff, murdered); Al Capone; Pope Pius X; Empress Eugénie of France; the Duke and Duchess of Windsor; and Nixon!

With lots of love to you and Sami and all good wishes for 1979,

Jeffrey

PS: Went to "Studio 54" twice – the grand hotel de luxe of discotheques – it deserves its high reputation. Loved Central Park –so exotic - I kept recalling Scott Fitzgerald's quote from "The Great Gatsby":-

"I love New York on summer afternoons when everyone's away. There's something very sensuous about it - overripe, as if all sorts of funny fruits were going to fall into your hands." That's how I felt.

PSS: Two Thai royals, a brother and a sister had the flat above yours in Oakley Street last summer, but they've gone back now.

14 Montagu Square
London W1H 1RD
26ᵗʰ October1979

Dear Beatrice,

Thanks for your letter and the article on King Vittorio
Emanuelle – I was very pleased with the interesting photos.
*   Well, I'm going into exile! London has changed too*
much – it's not the place it was in the early 70's – far from
it. I'll be living in Paris until spring, maybe longer, then
I hope to move to New York. I love Manhattan. I spent
six weeks there last year and five this summer. I expect you
will be in the States by the time I get there, so I'll let you
know when I hope to arrive. It will be fun living in the
same country again and I hope we'll see a lot of each other.
*   With lots of love to you and Sami*

Yours,
Jeffrey

So much was unsaid in this letter. It was clear that Jeffrey did not want to discuss the details of his betrayal.

Beatrice understood how courageous Jeffrey was to maintain his dignity in the aftermath of the pirating of his cherished work. No mention was made of his health. Was he recovering at this new address in Montegue Square?

Beatrice and Sami and their young family were returning to the States the following year with great apprehension. In the six years they had lived in Italy friendships had been established, a great love of Italian culture and language had flourished, Daniela was fluent not only in Italian but also in the local dialect acquired at her asilo nido. Sami had completed his degree but would have to acquire a State License to practice. It was clear that they were all beginning a new uncertain chapter in their lives.

USA 1980-1982

The journey back to the States was thwarted with difficulty. Sami had graduated from the Veterinary School but he had to jump through the multiple bureaucratic hoops on their return to the States in order to become licensed. In fact, that was not accomplished for five harrowing years. Beatrice had not completed her courses and there were vague plans of returning to complete the degree in Medicine. Reluctantly they relinquished their life in Italy and took up residence for a year in Ithaca New York, Cornell University being renowned for Veterinary Medicine. Living outside of the town on seven acres of land they settled into a comfortably furnished house. Two kittens were presented as a gift by the landlord to the children who named them Snug and Hug. Four chickens were acquired and Sami built a coop for them before setting off back to Bologna to receive his official papers. In the meantime, Beatrice had gathered a small circle of friends gleaned from the playgroups of the children. Autumn had arrived and over the two months that Sami was away she settled the family into a comforting routine.

Circo arrived triumphant with Sami. His first act was to devour one of the free-range chickens, after all he was a hunting dog. From then on he remained chained and took on his original purpose of guarding the family, although in Ithaca there was little danger of being kidnapped

Beatrice informed Sami, "we have seven acres of land and a barn and I have decided to acquire a pony for the children." Completing her studies was no longer guaranteed and she wanted to take the opportunity to fulfill one of her dreams. Based on an advert in the local paper Beatrice bought a pony described as "too old for the family." He was knobbly-knee'd and rather ugly but she liked his warm intelligent eyes. They named him "Welshtail." Over the winter his legs straightened out and by early spring, as his winter coat was shed, a magnificent young stallion emerged. A tooth fell out. "Sami, come quickly, he has lost a tooth!" "Well my dear, you apparently acquired a foal and now look at him, he is a real beauty."

Welshtail was highly spirited and would chase the children but did not mess with Beatrice. They had an understanding.

The kittens had kindled the desire of a local tomcat and soon delivered between them nine kittens. Daniela and Gabriele were thrilled. Culling the brood was out of the question.

By the summer of 1981 they were on the move again with an interim stay in New York City. The children had never before lived in an apartment. After four hellish weeks of heat, humidity, dragging the kids to playgrounds, which were not conveniently nearby, and worrying about their future, Sami accepted with great relief a job offered in the Catskill Mountains.

No letters were exchanged between Jeffrey and Beatrice during this period of turmoil and upheaval.

They moved to Broadlands early August 1981 where Sami took up his duties as Assistant live-in Veterinarian for the racehorses being bred on the farm. A consortium of businessmen had bought a magnificent parcel of land from the estate of one of the descendants of Elbridge Gerry, who had been one of the signers of the United States Declaration of Independence and the Articles of Confederation.

The area was breathtakingly beautiful. Unpaved roads crisscrossed this huge tract of land of two thousand acres, one of which led to a vast luxurious stable. Built in stone with rafters of hefty wood that had been weathered over the years displaying a patina of durability, it housed the thoroughbreds in spacious boxes, detailed with brass hinges and wrought iron gratings, names and provenance etched on polished brass plaques affixed to the individual doors. On entering the stable yard under an impressive Victorian-style brick arch was found the managers' house contiguous to the stable.

Before arriving at the stable complex a fork in the road snaked its way through luxuriant foliage. Each side of the path was lined with towering trees before opening up into an elegant circular driveway from which one glimpsed the grand façade of the mansion.

On the estate various cottages and barns were scattered about and vast fields, populated with thoroughbred mares and foals, stretched over the hills as far as the eye could see.

A white owl guarded the entrance to this magical land, perched predictably on the same branch of a tree overlooking his domain.

The family took over a dilapidated two story wooden house. In front of the kitchen window was a small paddock and behind that was a lopsided barn with two broken down stalls. Beyond that extended a vista of beauty, the kind of which quietens the soul suppressing anxiety and haunts one for the rest of one's life.

The family was reunited with Welshtail and the large feline family, but the chickens had been given away to friends who would appreciate the fresh eggs and promise not to eat the chickens. Beatrice had become particularly fond of her chickens since they had kept good company when Sami had been away. Circo was no longer with them. He had disappeared one day in Ithaca and they feared that a local farmer may have shot him, an inglorious end for a faithful dog.

Daniela was signed up for kindergarten in the hamlet of Andes. A school bus would pick her up just halfway along the dirt road to their house. This entailed a mile and a half walk twice a day to a remote spot where the rickety old bus would arrive and could turn back without too much difficulty to the main road. It became a challenging journey by foot after the arrival of the first snow in October.

A companion was found for Welshtail. Joey was a two-year old gelding Standardbred used for harness racing. Since he would always break out of the trot and start cantering, he was no longer useful to the owners. His arrival completed their 'family.' He was well behaved, gentle and eager to learn.

Of the many visitors who braved the journey to their remote post, Jeffrey was the first to arrive.

Jeffrey had put together, from his extensive archives, a fascinating book on the European Royal Families packed with unique photographs accompanied by interesting anecdotes. It was to be published in the States and for that purpose Jeffrey was in New York, settling into a large shabby studio in the West 70's with a sweeping view of the Hudson River.

Aware that Jeffrey would be in England for the 'Wedding of the Century,' he was invited to visit upon his return at the end of the summer.

Beatrice was impatient to hear from him and always grabbed the letters from Sami whenever he returned from the village Post Office. On this particular day a letter arrived from her sister Janet back in Liverpool and she eagerly tore open the envelope to soak up news from a more sophisticated life. A newspaper cutting fluttered to the floor. Puzzled, the only article in its entirety was highlighted by the photograph of a car being pulled up vertically by a crane from a canal. Gradually the names materialized in the body of the text, "Businessman Stanley Finestone and his wife Freda in tragic accident."

Enveloped in a cold shiver of horror, Beatrice screamed, "Look after the children," as she threw the letter at Sami. She ran out to the paddock and jumped onto Joey and galloped off, blinded by tears.

As the afternoon wound down she had managed to suppress the anguish invoked by this dreadful news and was able to return back to her duties at home.

Now more composed and with the children in bed, they could talk. "I don't believe it was an accident," announced Beatrice. "Nor do I" agreed Sami. Over a glass of wine they sat on the crumbling porch steps and talked quietly.

"Last time I was in England Aunt Freda was highly distressed and appeared to be in the throes of a breakdown. She was inconsolable recounting the death of a newborn during the Blitz. You remember me telling you how embarrassed Uncle Stanley was?" Sami nodded, "You English are so reserved and stoic, it seems that your aunt was not allowed to grieve at the time." "So much so," replied Beatrice, "that none of us even knew about it."

Now they waited with anxiety for Jeffrey's visit. How was he going to cope? What could they say? Would he have the same suspicions?

It was the last week of August. Jeffrey arrived late afternoon as the sun was setting behind the mountains. Sami had picked him up from the bus stop in Andes. As he emerged from the car the tribe of kittens scattered in all directions except for the one with the speckled grey and white coat, "I was thinking of having a cat to keep me company in the city," said Jeffrey vaguely. They moved indoors as swarms of gnats hovered in their dance at dusk, the birds already perched on the branches of the tree in front of the house, twittering gaily as if heralding the arrival of their guest. Inside the warmth of the kitchen, Jeffrey introduced himself politely to the children and presented each with a newly minted coin set commemorating the Royal Wedding. He appeared to be holding out and to be in good cheer. After offering their condolences, any talk about his parents was avoided that evening. Beatrice did notice that he was wearing a jacket bearing the ritual tear on the lapel, symbolic of grief for a loved one.

Dinner was consumed, the children put to bed and Jeffrey accompanied Beatrice to bed down the horses. In the mudroom adjoining the house, a large cup was filled with grain and Beatrice grabbed off the lid of the container what she thought was the torch. They sauntered out into the deep darkness of a moonless night. To their intense amusement they realized that instead of a torch Beatrice had grabbed a carrot! Weakened with laughter and being somewhat inebriated they were barely able to retrace their steps back to the mudroom to search for the torch. Back on track, in the glowing circle of light, Beatrice noticed the gray and white kitten at the heels of Jeffrey. "You have found your cat, or rather you have been found by him."

Jeffrey took his visit seriously, dignifying the local and only diner on the main street with his observations. They sat by the window, across from the firehouse. Looking around at the walls decorated with faded lacquered newspaper print, decades old, Jeffrey sat back and remarked that he was dining in the "best joint in town."

Beatrice had been given the key to the mansion to do her laundry using the industrial sized machines in the lower levels. Jeffrey accompanied her the next day for this weekly chore. As the machines rumbled with the load of washing and did their work, Beatrice took Jeffrey on a tour. From the entrance hall one passed by the butler's office, still lined with a pigeon-holed cabinet and rows of keys. The ground floor was extensive with an impressively grand lounge, a wood paneled dining room, two kitchens, one of which had vast walk-in freezers to hang the carcasses of deer, some guest bedrooms and a huge games room with a vast billiard table. A discrete staircase to the right of the hallway led up to the servants' wing with a warren of small rooms containing bare iron bedsteads. In contrast, the guest bedrooms in the main house were ready for use: sheets and blankets on the beds, soap and towels in the adjacent bathrooms. The lounge and dining room were also fully furnished and the walls bore countless old oil paintings. Jeffrey squealed in delight recognizing some of the artists' names. "My goodness, these must be worth a fortune," he exclaimed. They parked themselves in the lounge and looked out of the majestic French windows to admire the view. An elegant terrace led to a perfectly designed lawn encircled by a thick copse of trees. It was not too difficult to imagine sophisticated gatherings of guests spilling out beyond the terrace to play croquet and admire the view of distant mountain ranges.

Dominating the room was an intact tiger skin with stuffed head almost lifting itself off from the floor, lips pulled back to reveal snarling teeth ready for the kill. There were clusters of small tables surrounded by comfortable armchairs. Despite all the furniture the room remained spacious and elegant. A side table next to Beatrice had a transparent plastic covered document lying casually on top. On all the previous washing excursions, she had sat at the same spot without noticing it. A brief glance revealed it was a copy of the Constitution of America and there was the name of Eldridge Gerry along with all the other signatures. Jeffrey was intrigued. Not quite royalty, but with Burke's Peerage he had been involved with the discussion about putting out a version with the genealogies of American Presidents: "Burke's Presidential Families of the USA" published 1975. Looking over his shoulder, as he read through the document, she noticed there was a mention of Judge Jeffries. Also known as 'The Hanging Judge', he was born in Wales 1645 and died 1689 in the Tower of London. His name was evoked by the Framers of The Constitution because it was known that judges could not always be trusted to safeguard the rights of the people and so served as a reminder. At the mention of his name cousin Jeffrey visibly bristled with anger and the mood in the light-filled salon shifted. "My parents always called me Judge Jeffries," he said bitterly, "and they didn't care to know that he had a terrible reputation for harsh sentencing." Then he carefully placed the document back on the table, clasped his hands together and fixing his eyes on her said, "Do you know how my parents died?" Chilled, she answered carefully, reciting the official verdict of the newspaper. "Let me tell you something Beatrice, their death was not accidental and I will tell you why." A gloom suffused the room. In the brief ensuing silence, as Beatrice waited for him to continue, she hoped that his story would not match the one she and Sami had imagined. With a sad resigned voice he continued. "As you know the so-called accident occurred the day after the Wedding. The neighbours reported that for the first time since moving into the flat two years earlier, my mother was animated and smiling. My father was taking her to her weekly chiropodist appointment. Somehow he ended up driving down a towpath by a canal. At a certain point he lowered the window to ask two men working on their barge which direction to take. They pointed back to the road from which he had strayed. My father thanked them politely, rolled up the window, turned the car to face the canal directly and drove straight in." Beatrice did not want to hear anymore but he continued relentlessly. "The car bobbed up and down in the water as the men shouted repeatedly, with violent gestures, to get my father to lower the window so that they could be hauled out. Apparently my father sat still with a slight smile and then raised his hands in a gesture of hopelessness, whilst my mother screamed in absolute terror. These men believed without doubt it was a deliberate action. I have interviewed them both in person. When the police went to their flat they found, in the middle of the lounge on the floor amongst all the crates of belongings that were never unpacked from their previous home, an open box containing the Will. By the phone, the address book was propped open at the page where I could be found. My parents knew that after the Wedding I had left London and was traveling up North to see them, staying overnight in Birmingham with my friend who takes care of my archives." He stopped briefly. "Oh Jeffrey," she sighed, "maybe——." Jeffrey raised his hand to silence her. "At the Funeral Home I demanded to see them before they were buried. My father looked peaceful, whereas my mother's expression was fixed in a mask of terror."

Beatrice whispered, "What does Robert say?" Jeffrey grimaced. "Robert was found by the police in a magic circle up in the Scottish Highlands with his friends from the commune, where he lives courtesy of the Laird's daughter. He believes only that they were fortunate to have died together in an accident."

The room was now dark and there was a heavy cloak of silence. They wept in each other's arms. There was nothing more to say.

—m—

The grey and white kitten adopted Jeffrey who named him Harlequin.

Beatrice and Jeffrey were to travel down to New York together. They were embarking on their next adventure.

Janet, the sister of Beatrice, had accompanied her close friend Cynthia Lennon to New York for an art gallery opening. Fifteen original drawings executed by Cynthia recalling her time with John

Lennon and The Beatles "done by memory for history" were to be shown. They were sketches done for her 1978 book 'A Twist of Lennon.' Cynthia's son Julian had been the invited guest but she was frightened to bring him after the brutal assassination of her ex-husband the year before. Instead, she invited her friend Janet. The opening of the exhibit was to take place in Southampton over Labour Day Weekend. An invitation was reluctantly procured for Jeffrey and Beatrice. It would be the only chance for Beatrice to see her sister since the transatlantic visit was brief.

Explicit instructions were given for the care of Welshtail and Joey. Daniela and Gabriele helped find a box for Harlequin. They had thoroughly enjoyed the visit of their second cousin and they were delighted that one of the kittens had found a good home.

On arriving in the city they parted ways; Beatrice set off to stay with Sami's uncle on the Upper East Side; Jeffrey, proudly bearing his box with the kitten, headed to the Upper West Side. The next day they met at Jeffrey's hairdresser. Her neglected hair, kept in a long untidy plait, was cut and shaped expertly. Champagne was offered and Jeffrey peeled her grapes from a large crystal glass bowl.

Later that day they set off from Grand Central Station to take the train to Southampton. Neither had experienced the Labour Day weekend exodus before and they were unprepared for the mass of people merrily bound in the same direction. After finding seats, Jeffrey blurted out, "I must find a smoking carriage," as he dashed off. Recalling how she had lost him at Ascot, Beatrice leapt up, gripping her overnight bag and promptly fell over a huge canvas bag blocking the passageway. As she was helped up by a considerate passenger, she realized that she had injured her knee. Limping off to the next carriage she found Jeffrey already seated, cigarette lit, held artfully between fingers. "Oh, there you are," he said gaily. Trying to be civil, Beatrice thought she would never forgive him if she were permanently damaged, rubbing her left knee, which was already swelling up and throbbing.

Janet and Cynthia were staying with the two men who owned the gallery, at an ultra-modern villa with swimming pool and a huge patio. It was made clear that Beatrice and Jeffrey were not welcome to stay the night. Taking her sister aside Beatrice asked if any arrangements had been made for them. She had no idea, being a guest herself. Well, it was too late to worry. As night fell they all set out to The Tower Gallery. Cynthia was a big attraction and a sufficiently impressive group of paparazzi snapped their cameras and thrust microphones in her direction. Janet was thrilled, edging her way into the photo shoot. Jeffrey and Beatrice hung back not wanting to be part of the circus.

The Tower Gallery had three levels and as they climbed up the spiral staircase they passed paintings by Lichtenstein on one level followed by Warhols on the next level and finally the sketches by Cynthia. The staircase continued up onto the roof where, the weather being clement, there was an outdoor reception. Forgetting that they had nowhere to sleep that night, Jeffrey and Beatrice found themselves being driven to a magnificent mansion on the beach known as The Ark. The open plan allowed the milling crowd to flow effortlessly around a huge banquet laid out on a massive central table. Large glass doors slid open onto the terrace from which steps led down to the beach where gigantic speakers amplified the music, overpowering the crashing boom of waves of the Atlantic Ocean. Observing the guests, Jeffrey began to look uncomfortable and hung closer to his cousin's side. He insisted that she accompany him to the bathroom and wait outside. A group of elegant men kept asking her when her husband would be coming out, casting acerbic looks at her as if they wished her to evaporate leaving the coast clear. Jeffrey steered her out onto the terrace whispering that he knew some of these men from previous visits to the States and didn't care for them. Scrambling down from the terrace, past the amplifiers they walked on the beach finally perching on a rock and silently watched the waves pounding the sand. Jeffrey fidgeted a bit trying to find the 'mot juste.' Then he looked up and said, "Beatrice, I have something serious to confess." She knew that the moment had finally arrived. "I am a homosexual." He looked at her wearily as if unsure of her reaction. She took his hand, threading her fingers through his. "Oh Jeffrey, you are silly. I have always known, even before I knew what it actually meant." He was so relieved that he became quite animated. "You know my parents never talked about girls. I was in a boarding school with just boys, as you well know." "How was it for you? You were so young." Immersed in his memories he murmured, "Well matron was wonderful, she used to tuck us in at night." Then wistfully he pronounced "If only my mother had talked to me about marriage."

Beginning to feel the chilled night air and recognizing fatigue setting in, they hatched a plan to tackle sleeping quarters. Beatrice suggested asking if they could stay at the mansion. "It looks as if there is enough room." Jeffrey wouldn't hear of it. Evidently he had had an unpleasant experience with this particular crowd in the past. Spotting Cynthia, he asked if she might have any influence finding a place for them. One of her hosts finally understood their dilemma, but did not want to upset his companion by bringing them back to their place. He produced the key to the Tower, "You can sleep there." He drove them over and dropped them off. Giggling, they entered the darkened gallery, stumbled up the staircase and grandly asked themselves the important question of the night. "Shall we sleep with Lichtenstein or Warhol?" The decision was helped by the fact that the Warhol floor had some straw matting. Separated by a small Japanese pool defined by a few pebbles, they fell into a deep sleep without the comfort of blankets or pillows. In the morning, stiff with cold, they found the bathroom and freshened up. Venturing out onto the main street of Southampton they found a nearby café and lingered over coffee and croissants until it was a more suitable hour to call the villa. They were picked up reluctantly and after saying their farewells were driven to the train station.

Back in New York, Beatrice stayed on another day. Jeffrey was invited for dinner at Sami's uncle's house. It happened that Sami's mother was visiting her brother. With watchful calculating eyes she had examined Jeffrey carefully. Taking Beatrice aside, she feigned great concern. "Do you know that he is wearing the jacket he wore for the funeral?" Referring to the cut lapel she shook her head mournfully, "That is bad luck." With her guttural middle-eastern accent, the pronouncement chilled Beatrice to the marrow.

Riverside Studios
Apt 7C8
342 West 71st Street,
New York, NY 10023
8th September 1981

Dear Beatrice,

I hope you got back home alright– it was a crazy weekend!
I'm going to spend the next few weeks getting back into my old routines, but I can't get over ending up six weeks of roving by sitting on a beach, with music and champagne, and partying with you, after all this time!
I've written to Robert and told him that he must stay with you when he comes to New York– I'm sure he will.
I'll let you know when I've seen Dieter

Lots of love
Jeffrey

Beatrice asked herself 'who was Dieter?" Maybe someone they had met at the party.

Apt 7C8
342 West 71ˢᵗ St.,
NY 10023
5ᵗʰ. October 1981

Dear Beatrice,

    Thanks for the lovely tin of tea which arrived just as I was finishing off my Chinese tea from London – wondering what to do about finding something to replace it!
    The book will be out on Thursday. Brentanos have featured it in their Christmas catalogue. Still waiting for the leaflets from London.
    On Wednesday night there will be a gala charity concert at Carnegie Hall for the Queen Frederika of Greece Memorial Fund and I am to present a copy of the book to the Governor and Mrs. Carey at the reception afterwards. Some royals will be coming including Princess Marie-Loire of Bulgaria and Prince Nikita Romanoff (he wasn't going to attend, but when he heard about the presentation decided he ought to show up to give me some "royal support"). His wife knows Robert Massie and said she'd like to give a party for us, as the publisher isn't going to give one – but it will be a small affair in her apartment.
    I started work last Thursday – I'm running a canteen for the staff of the Brooklyn Academy of Music – 9 to 3 each day and good pay and food.
    Lots of love to Sami and the children.

Love,
Jeffrey

The title of the book was **"The Last Courts of Europe: A Royal Family Album 1860-1914."** It featured a compendium of eccentric, poignant photographs of Europe's vanishing and endangered Royal families culled from Jeffry's archives. The collection had taken off at the beginning of his passion for royalty, when Jeffrey wrote to all the deposed royals of Europe. At that time, the late 50's and early 60's, it appears they were only too happy to be remembered and plied Jeffrey with photos and anecdotes. Aunt Freda had once proudly shown Beatrice the extension to the bungalow built to accommodate the growing volume of albums. Incidentally Beatrice did notice that not only had the royals taken up residence but also an abundance of potted tomato vines nurtured by her uncle Stanley.

Two book covers were printed. One was for the American market where the name of Robert Massie was prominent. He had written the prologue and being a household name was deemed more suitable. The cover for the British edition featured, more accurately, Jeffrey's name.

New York
21ˢᵗ.October 1981

Dear Beatrice,

Thanks for your letter. So glad you like the book.
   Have broken the sad news of the ginger kitten's death to his sibling Harlequin, who just grows and grows.

Lots of love,
Jeffrey

—〽—

Riverside Studios
Apt 7C8,
342 West 71ˢᵗ. Street,
New York, NY 10023

Dear Beatrice and Sam,

At last the leaflets!
 I'm expecting Robert some time this month, but don't have a date yet.
 After he leaves I shall start getting ready to leave for the Far East – there are now three big royal events coming up, and two of them are in Bangkok where I shall be heading to anyway. I might leave by Christmas, or soon after.
 Beginning to get worried about Harlequin. New York being what it is I don't seem to be able to find anyone to give him to and I don't want to hand him over to a neighbour. Perhaps it might be a good thing if he went back to Andes. Would you want him back? If so your next visit to New York would be as good a time as any. He's growing very fast and is full of energy – really too much for just one room. He seems very tough and in need of exercise. When I let him into the corridor he tears off at great speed and runs up and down like a bullet!
 Do keep in touch won't you.

Lots of love,
Jeffrey

In November Robert undertook the pilgrimage to Andes. Winter had come early and since October the ground had been well covered with snow. Braving the blast of cold air, Robert emerged from the bus with a broad smile lighting up his face, clutching the collar of his inadequate jacket in an attempt to stave off the biting wind.

Robert had left his Scottish commune to try out the New World, his destination being Peru.

It was the hunting season and it was imperative that the horses did not get loose, since the hunters would shoot at anything that moved in the woods, including people. The weekend that Robert arrived, Joey was mistakenly turned out at the same time as Welshtail. If one was in the barn the other would hang around, but with both of them on the loose they quickly disappeared from view. Panicking, Beatrice set off for the Stables, a favourite spot for them. They were nowhere in sight. It was getting dark and, despondent, the family sat in the kitchen around the wood heated stove, wondering what to do next. Robert, with a barely perceptible stutter, requested a piece of string and a sketch of the farm. He fashioned a primitive pendant and swung it over the crude rendition of a map. Gleeful, he leaped up and grabbing his hosts exclaimed, "drive me this direction." He pointed to the path that led to the contiguous estate of the remaining Gerry family. Skeptical, the family piled into the car, the children subdued. Ten minutes away, there they were, heads hanging over the fencing of a small paddock next to a derelict cottage. Beatrice had renewed respect for her cousin's strange ways.

Sami drove Robert back to New York and meeting up with Jeffrey treated the two brothers to lunch at Tavern on the Green: a memorable event for all concerned.

Entering the month of December it was clear that things were not working out on the farm. Tensions were growing. In the midst of this uncertainty, Jeffrey and Beatrice had a huge fight. "Come and pick up Harlequin," he ordered down the phone. Beatrice had found herself saying "leave him on the street." The words escaped unchecked since she would never commit such a heinous act herself. Jeffrey was rightly infuriated, "how on earth could you suggest such a thing?" Chastened, Sami and Beatrice drove down to the city and received the adored companion of her cousin. They graciously agreed to give him a daily shiastu massage and keep his opulent coat well groomed. He was twice as big as the other grown kittens and clearly spoilt.

With a heavy heart Beatrice embraced her beloved cousin. She felt deep within her soul that they would never meet again. Sami tried to reassure her. But she had no doubt that her instincts were correct, as illogical as it might seem.

Jeffrey left for his new life in the Far East after spending some time in Paris.

After the New Year, the family visited New York. As they walked down Fifth Ave, Beatrice was proud to note that all the bookstores had stacked pyramids of Jeffrey's book prominently displayed in the windows.

"The Last Courts of Europe" was a huge success. It was awarded the History Book of the Month award.

1982-88

9

The ensuing years were catastrophic. Beatrice and Sami were confronted with seemingly insurmountable problems, which they waded through only to encounter further traumas. But by the end of the 80's they emerged shell-shocked but viable. There was a scarcity of letters from Jeffrey. On rereading them Beatrice could detect an underlying melancholy and wistfulness. He was traveling his own painful vicissitudes of life.

Nonetheless, Jeffrey's years in the Far East until his untimely death in 1997 were immensely productive. He completed two scholarly books on the Genealogy of the Thai Royal Family, wrote innumerable articles on various East Asian Royals and completed a book, unfortunately not published until after his demise, on the monarchies of South East Asia.

By the end of January1982 the unwinterized ramshackle house finally defeated them. As wind sheared through gaping holes in the wood plank walls, the children abandoned their upstairs bedrooms and joined their parents around the wood heated stove in the kitchen. At night the stove needed feeding at least twice which rapidly depleted the once mountainous stockpile of chopped wood. When the pipes froze, Beatrice learnt that a huge pot of snow melted down to an inch of water. She learnt that once the brooks and streams froze solid the horses did eat snow, contrary to local belief. Finally, they all learnt that performing bathroom duties outside in temperatures of minus 20 degrees Farenheit was not to be taken lightly.

They moved down to the village on the corner of route 28, the "milk route,' and bore out another one and a half years in less than comfortable circumstances. The diminutive apartment on the second floor of a two-story building faced a one-room Post Office across the courtyard. No more trekking for letters. A stream behind the building became, in the spring, a friendly gurgling flow of crystal-clear water destined for the reservoirs of New York City. The school was now just across the street. They counted their blessings.

One frigid night, not long after resettling themselves, Sami and Beatrice rode the horses down from the farm to an empty cow barn just around the corner from their building. A full moon bathed the unlit country road. Sami rode Welshtail who was equipped with an oversized saddle, which kept slipping around his belly hindering a much-needed haste to minimize exposure in the punishing cold. Sensing the importance of the event both horses began neighing with long drawn-out sounds, which reverberated across the valley. Although the barn was accessible to thirty-seven acres of land it was unsuitable for pleasure riding being stony and very steep. But the horses were their family, as Beatrice would explain to the kids whenever they revolted against helping out every evening with their bedding down in the barn. During the day they were let loose on the vast acreage of stony fields where an ample stream provided water. At sunset Beatrice, after placing the kids in a safe spot in the barn, would meet up with the "family' who would be waiting at the decrepit gate salivating for the container of oats and bale of fresh hay waiting for them. No need to attach a lead to their halters. Once the gate was unlatched they would gallop at top speed down the short slope leading to the barn and careen to a stop in front of their allotted spots. As they guzzled up their oats they would be groomed by the children before leaving them for the night. Many a day the doorbell would ring and standing by the doorway, at the foot of the stairs leading up to the apartment, would be a considerate neighbour with the two 'naughty boys' returning them after their escape from the poorly fenced land.

Sami eventually found a job in New York City visiting his family occasionally. Beatrice's days were full. Daniela continued to attend the local school and Gabriele joined a local crèche allowing Beatrice enough time to drive to Delhi and study in the library for a few hours trying to keep alive the fading goal of completing her medical degree. She also managed to be given an unofficial externship by a compassionate doctor in the local Delhi Hospital where she spent time in the Emergency Room and Operating Room given simple duties thus stoking her will to persist in her studies.

Then Sami organized taking care of the children for six weeks whilst Beatrice returned back to Bologna in 1982, for the first time since her departure, to take an exam. During her visit she found a room that would remain available throughout the following three years.

On her return from this first visit, one exam successfully completed, Gabriele did not immediately recognize her! He had never spent a day without her. Although the incident of him recoiling from her was brief it was sobering and prompted Beatrice to question the wisdom of pursuing a dream at the expense of one's children.

—⟋⟋⟍—

Liverpool, 15th August 1982

Dear Beatrice,

Arrived back in England the day before you wrote from Italy and have spent the last four weeks traveling around. I went over to the flat for the first time a couple of days ago and was very happy to find your nice letter.

After all we didn't have the stone setting, as your father made so many complications that in the end I had to call things to a halt from Malaysia around the middle of

June. However, Robert came over anyway, and we spent the anniversary together in St. Annes, which seemed so much more fitting. He returned to Bolivia a few days ago and I am now in Liverpool 'chez Janet'.

I shall be going over to Paris at the end of the month and have decided to settle there for the time being. Don't have an address yet.

The trip was quite amazing – in fact I spent all the time from February till July in Thailand, Malaya and Singapore - when I arrived back in London I'd circumnavigated in less than 12 months.

I spoke to your mother and Aunty Betty about Odessa and neither of them admitted to knowing anything about Grandma coming from there.

Can you remember where you heard about it – I'm very curious and want to get to the bottom of it.

When I arrived back in London I had great difficulty in adjusting to the time difference of seven hours and was in fact sleeping less and less each night, until I eventually fainted in the street – when I got to hospital, where I spent a few days, they told me I'd had an epileptic fit. They suggested that this could have been brought on by falling down and thought that after six months in the tropics I was probably exhausted. Can you let me know whether its possible that the fit was caused this way? Also, any more information on Dupuytren's syndrome.

Until I have an address in Paris you can write to me,

c/o Monsieur Max Karkegi.
30 rue Gregoire de Tours,
F-75006 Paris

With lots of love to Sami and the children
Love
Jeffrey

Beatrice never found out the cause of Jeffreys' disaffection with her father: yet another unsolved mystery in the typical family fashion of silence. From then on Jeffrey communicated with Beatrice's father via cousin Ruth, daughter of the solicitor Arthur.

She was alarmed over his health problems. Her aunt Freda had talked to Beatrice about having Dupuytren's syndrome, showing her the crooked fingers. Heredity plays a part and indeed there is a connection to epilepsy but no more episodes were reported so she reassured him and herself that fatigue was most likely responsible.

Mr. Karkegi, Jeffrey's host in Paris, turned out to be a well-known authority on Egyptian Royalty.

c/o Monsieur Max Karkegi,
30 rue Gregoire de Tours,
F-75006 Paris

19th January 1983

Dear Mr. Jones,

Following your request to Mr. M. Field for instructions regarding the erection of a tombstone for the late Mr. and Mrs. S.H. Finestone, I enclose herewith the English wording for the tombstone.

The memorial required is No. 2 (white marble memorial), with white marble cover slab (double size) as per your letter to Mr. Field of 3rd April 1982. The price quoted then was 710 pounds for the stone and 132 pounds for the cover – I understand from Mr. Field that the price has now risen. I would be obliged if you would now proceed with the erection of the stone, and submit your account to Messrs. Beacon and Beacon, Solicitors, 30 Hamilton Square, Birkenhead, Merseyside L41 6 AZ (for the attention of Mrs. Yates).

Upon erection the stone should be covered until such time as a service and dedication can be arranged.

Yours sincerely,
J. Finestone

—〜〜—

c/o Mr. Max Karkegi
19th January 1983

Dear Ruth,

Enclosed here with copy of instructions to Messrs Aimud J.Jones.

I have written to Robert asking him whether he will be able to return this summer to be present at the service.

I have amended the wording of the inscription to include brothers and sisters, as was suggested in August, but have left the rest of the inscription almost as it was, as Rev. Dr. Jacobs told us that he had no objection to it as it stood, although it was somewhat unusual, and of course the Hebrew inscription will be in complete conformity with orthodox usage.

I have started looking for a studio and am most anxious to get settled as quickly as possible, for apart from the hardship and expense of living in a one-star Parisian hotel, I have just started work on my new book and am unable to proceed with the work as I would wish in the present conditions. Moreover, I shall have to undertake a research trip to Asia to complete the work, and this will not be possible unless I first get myself settled in comfortable accommodation,

With all good wishes to you and your family

Love
Jeffrey

Ruth then forwarded this letter to Beatrice's father.

By the spring of 1983 Sami had received a temporary license from the State of New Jersey. He stayed with his brother in Princeton looking for a place to live and a job.

In '82 and '83, prior to the change in location, Beatrice had made a couple of forays to Bologna. On the first occasion the children were left in the care of Sami. The second time, since Sami was working again in New York, they were put up by the local artists they had befriended who had a daughter the same age as Gabriele. Embarking on her third trip Daniela and Gabriele were shipped off to Evanston Illinois, the residence of Sami's parents. They were still there when Beatrice returned, from Italy, another exam in the pocket. She flew directly to Chicago and endured the pitying looks and whispered asides, referring to her and Sami's dismal lives, between the various family members gathered for the summer. After a flurry of phone calls from Sami, suffering similar inequities under the auspices of his older brother, he finally requested that she meet him back in Andes having found a house and a job in New Jersey. They were to move lock, stock and barrel, placing Joey and Welshtail in a riding school further up North. An attrition of their feline population had occurred via kidnapping (Harlequin and their favourite, Tuxedo, the most charismatic, were 'acquired' by the estate workers) and from raccoon attacks. They were left with Snug and Hug and two remaining offspring.

The new home was adequate. Built on a new estate on land which had once been a potato farm, the countryside was perceptible at the periphery. Princeton was the nearest town making the blandness of the area more palatable. In fact Beatrice took advantage of the esteemed McCarter Theatre which provided many edifying events, not least the annual Nutcracker performance at Christmas. The very day the children arrived from Chicago to join them another carpet was pulled from under their feet. New Jersey State rules had changed and there was now no longer a temporary license, therefore no job! When the shock wore off Sami reactivated his old teaching license and went back to New York to teach: a long commute.

However, the children settled in well. There were tennis courts and a swimming pool just walking distance away, and children to play with. Daniela started ballet classes in the nearby town of Cranbury and both attended the esteemed Westminster School Music in Princeton for piano lessons. Once they were signed up for school Beatrice set off again for three weeks in Bologna. A surprisingly competent au pair from the Virgin Islands was left in charge of the household.

25 rue du Sommerard,
F-75005 Paris.

4th October 1983

Dear Beatrice,

Lovely to receive your news, and thanks for the article on Princess Elizabeth of Toro – one of my favourite royals. I met her in Uganda and was terribly impressed – can remember Amin's interest in her the day we left when she appeared at the airport in hot pants to say goodbye to us all – but she stayed behind and became foreign minister. Didn't see her again as she only moved to London after I left, but occasionally saw her sister, Princess Mabel (who lived up to her name and lacked her sister's beauty)– she once amused me by singing the national anthem of Toro for me – set to the music of Swaney River!!!!!!!

Well, now for the big news (but don't say anything when writing home as it will be a secret until after the event) – Robert is getting married to a Bolivian girl on 5th November. I'm flying out for the wedding later this month and will be accompanied by my cousin Janice Finestone. We shall be flying via Rio de Janeiro and will be stopping off there for a few days on the way back. How's that for a piece of news! I don't know much about my future sister-in-law other than that she is Bolivian Indian, Catholic, and that her name is Angelica. As Robert put it, it couldn't cause more consternation in Childwall if he announced his engagement to E.T. So we decided not to say anything until after the event, as we would hardly expect anyone to fly out to the wedding and feel it is best to wait until it has become fait accompli.

Was very interested to hear about your mother's dream – both Robert and I had dreams which suggested that Mummy is now at peace – though all three dreams are very different. Robert dreamt the night before the stone setting (after he planned to hold his own 'ceremony' in La Paz), that he was playing a tape recorder in the boudoir at Beverley Road, St. Annes (you remember the room adjoining the big bedroom, used as a dressing room) that Daddy came in from the bedroom and told him not to make so much noise as Mummy was sleeping – and not to disturb her – he took it to mean that he shouldn't try to make 'contact' the next day, and so he didn't. My dream was rather heavier. I was standing beside the shul in St. Annes and suddenly beneath it I saw an immense hall below ground level, which was a mausoleum. In all directions, but far off as the hall was so big, were countless coffins, which contained members of the family going back hundreds of years, and as I looked at the scene I understood that Mummy and Daddy's coffin was amongst them, and that they had now 'joined their ancestors' and were no longer able to communicate with me. I accepted the situation and woke up. I dreamt this a few days before the stone setting and after the ceremony felt very relieved to have it over with.

*If you do return to Italy, then you must come to Paris
on the way back and stay a few days – I have an extra
room. It would so much fun to be in Paris together. I'm
sure you'd enjoy it.*

*Glad to hear the last news of Harlequin – still think
about him.*

*Decided not to go to King Leopold's funeral – actually
there was a French royal funeral in Paris the same week –
a first cousin of King Leopald.*

Lots of love to Sami and the children

Love,
Jeffrey

Beatrice's mother, normally taciturn, had described to her the dream in which she had been sitting with her sister at home. She looked at peace and had reassured her mother that "all was well."

The furthest from Beatrice's mind was to organize a detour to Paris. She was ravaged by guilt for leaving her children with strangers, and she was emotionally drained by the rules and regulations imposed on her husband leaving them both devastated and fearful, barely hanging on to their dreams and goals. She lived under a dark cloud. But still, she bitterly regretted not having done so.

—⟋⟍—

25 rue du Sommerard,
F-75005 Paris.
(sent: Xmas 1983)

Dear Beatrice

Many thanks for your Christmas card.
Glad you were thrilled to hear about Robert's wedding.
Enclosed a couple of photos.

Robert's address is:-
P.O. Box 2822
La Paz

Bolivia

He doesn't have a home phone number.
I'm getting ready for another trip – to Brunei, for the Independence ceremonies next month – Prince Charles will attend and the Sultan is going to put on a big show.
I haven't any real news at present, so will sign off by sending all my love to you, Sami, Daniela and Gabriele, and wish you a happy and successful 1984.

Lots of love, Jeffrey

Joining his cousin Janice Finestone, Jeffrey had set off to La Paz Bolivia for his brother's wedding. The death of their parents had resulted in Robert and Jeffrey forging a bond between them, getting along amicably and effortlessly. As was his custom Jeffrey had viewed this marriage in the same light as a royal event, two dynasties combining together. Angelika became Mrs. Finestone wearing the wedding band of Jeffrey and Robert's mother.

Many years later Beatrice heard from Robert that "although Jeffrey found the altitude difficult to tolerate, suffering from the typical headaches and shortness of breath of mountain sickness, his acceptance of Angelica and her family was spontaneous and genuine. And Angelica fell under his spell as so many did, despite not having a language in common."

Paris, 15th July 1984
(sent: to Liverpool)

Dear Beatrice,

Lovely to receive your letter. Things sound as if they are pretty complicated in New Jersey. People seem to be very against foreigners, whatever country – not just America, though they have the biggest immigrant hang-up of all. An English friend of mine recently lost a job in Amsterdam – his employer remarked after he'd left – "that's the last time we employ a foreigner here' – he's Israeli!!, long settled in Holland, but really! Such attitude!

Glad to hear you'll be in Liverpool. Of course at this time of year I think a lot about Liverpool. For the first time in three summers I don't actually have to be there, so I'm not coming over to England this summer. Robert looks at it rather differently – he doesn't want to visit England during 1984 – I feel the same way too. The miner's strike must be making things a bit grim.

Please tell your parents I think of them a lot and give them my love. And of course Janet and Roy. The family seems to have broken up – cousin Freda didn't invite me to her son Anthony's wedding – and as he's married a French girl and the wedding was at the Chelsea Register Office on King's Road I'd probably have gone. I hear a whole charabanc went from Childwall. Please tell me all about it if you can.

I was in Brunei in February – for the independence ceremonies – Prince Charles was there. Also Adnan Khashoggi – would you believe I was asked onto his yacht, twice on the same day. The Sultan's new palace has 1200 rooms and is bigger than the Vatican – even bigger than that house on the beach at the Hamptons (imagine what I could have said to that girl when she asked us if we'd ever been in such a big house as the beach house – and I'd answered – yes, but in Europe). I spent a week at Raffles Hotel in Singapore on the way back – wonderful. Enclosed an article from the picturesquely named "Borneo Bulletin".

Beatrice – can you do me a big favour and get in touch with Janice Finestone. She's possibly coming over to Liverpool at the end of August with my photo album of Robert's wedding – to give to a Bolivian to take back as we don't want to post them. She might bring her slides with her, so you'd be able to see everything. If she doesn't come over while you are there, why not go over to St. Annes for the day with the children – she'd love to meet them. Actually Janice is going to tell Aunty Betty the big news from Bolivia - Angelica is expecting a baby – late September, early October. In case she hasn't, please tell everyone when you arrive. The name will be Freda Marcela or Juan Stanley.

Do write when you get to Liverpool and let me know all the news. I want to know how Uncle Peter, Aunty Ruth and Susan are.

Lots of love,
Jeffrey

The trip to England over the summer of '84 had followed after a big family gathering in Tel Aviv on the occasion of the barmitzvah of their nephew, son of one of Sami's sisters. Beatrice had taken the opportunity to make yet another attempt to knock off some exams in Bologna after escorting the kids and dropping them off at their grandparents in Liverpool. Janice did come with her amazing photographs of the wedding in La Paz. A slide show was set up in the dining room of her parent's house much to the consternation of Beatrice's mother who hid in the lounge and could be heard muttering "she must be turning in her grave." She was distraught that Angelika was now Mrs. Finestone and wearing her sister's wedding ring.

However, Beatrice believed her aunt Freda would have been thrilled to know that in the article on Jeffrey in the "Borneo Bulletin" of March 3rd 1984 it was noted how the late Lord Mountbatten had assisted him in his quest to write about the British Royal Family.

———ɯɯ———

25 rue du Sommerard
F-75005 Paris

13th October 1984

Dear Beatrice,

It was lovely receiving your letter and new year card – many thanks.

It was interesting reading your reflection on Liverpool. I know those two photos of the family in the early fifties - quite amazing. What strikes me about them is the formality of it all – the dress, the pose, the style of photography. Now the family, like so many others, no longer aspires to such style! Your comment on my parents reminded me of something. When I was clearing the house I came across their wedding portraits – I'd never seen them before – even when in 1966 I collected all the family pictures together to make an album! Mummy always kept them well hidden. They are photographically beautiful, but I know why she didn't like them – she has the most fearful haunted look on her face, especially in the close-up shots. Like her, I now keep them well out of sight and find it hard to look at them!

As I know you have heard, Robert is the proud father of a son, Juan Stanley, and I am a proud uncle. It's hard to think of Robert as a father, but I am sure he'll be a good one. And Angelica's a marvelous mother.

*By the way, Anthony phoned last week - he'll be in
Paris at the end of the month, with his wife, and we're all
to have dinner together with her parents, who are coming
up from the south.*

*I thought of you last weekend- I was at a ceremony
for the Royal Family of Laos, and for the first time met
one of the children of the Crown Prince – his second son,
now a strapping lad of 20. Still no news of his parents,
who we met at the Embassy- it looks as though the Crown
Prince has disappeared, though his wife is said to be living
quietly in the capital with her younger children – only the
two eldest are in France – they crossed into Thailand two
years ago with their old nurse (an ancient Princess who I
see often in Paris, and much to her amusement, chew betel
nut with – you get quite a high from it, which lasts 10-
15 minutes – the old Lao ladies chew it all the time – the
young ones laugh to see me chew it but I don't care – they
don't know what it does having never tried it).*

*Loved the story of Daniela and her tie. Quite right - if the
Princess of Wales wears one it must be correct!!*

*Write soon,
Lots of love to all,*

Jeffrey

The last time Beatrice had seen her Aunt Freda she was in a
dreadful state. On one her brief visits to England, the winter of '80,
her parents had driven her over for lunch at her aunt and uncle's
new home. Beatrice had been told by her mother, on a number of
occasions, that she was concerned about her sister but she hadn't
taken much note.

Uncle Stanley had made a disastrous decision to sell the house
with the view of the sea. Jeffrey had described once, with great

humour, that it was just too much for the two of them to make the daily decision of what to gather to take up to the lounge on the upper floor from the kitchen and bedroom on the ground floor. The new house turned out to be made of defective concrete. They were bankrupted. And so Aunt Freda left her beloved Victorian seaside resort where all the locals knew her well, to live in a small apartment far from the coast. Being close to one of her brothers offered no consolation. She plunged into a deep depression and after the translocation never unpacked her items.

Her aunt had moved around the cramped apartment in a daze, her face frozen in grief. Lunch consisted of soup from a can, lumpy from the added water. A far cry from the days when they would be offered fresh salmon and asparagus followed by strawberries and cream and possibly a deliciously rich chocolate cake made by Jeffrey if he happened to be home from school. In the lounge, surrounded by the unpacked crates, Aunt Freda embarked on the story of her first child born during the war at the height of the infamous blitz on Manchester in December 1940 by the German Luftwaffe. At the end of the pregnancy she suffered from eclampsia. Her obstetrician was unable to reach her because of the ferocity of bombs falling over the area. A perfectly formed baby boy was stillborn. In those days grief was not allowed to be expressed. It was deemed impolite to mourn over a dead baby and so she had suppressed her sorrow. Now she was making up for lost time. As she clasped and unclasped her slender hands and intertwined her delicate fingers she described in intimate detail her pain as Uncle Stanley sat expressionless with occasional tics crossing his impassive face betraying his concern over his wife's indiscretion.

Jeffrey and I had talked at length about this on the beach in Southhampton that summer of 1981. He was angry, even then. "My mother didn't tell me until I was 19 years old! I had never understood why I was always in such a hurry. Now I believe that the spirit of my dead brother was trying to return. If only I had known. It would have helped me understand their way of life and their peculiarities and about my own impatience and neurosis about time." He had continued with a note of sarcasm, "and do you know Beatrice, that my mother's favourite novel was Tolstoy's 'Anna Karenina' especially the ending when she throws herself under a train."

At some point in '84, Sami was rescued from his teaching job in New York City. A temporary position as New Jersey State Equine Epidemiologist and State Veterinarian, which did not require a license, had opened up. Visiting stables and farms across the state allowed Sami flexible hours. After long heated discussions he persuaded Beatrice to leave for Italy and not return until she graduated. The decision was weighted with an incredible pain at the reality of abandoning her children. An au pair was found, highly recommended by a respected Princeton family who knew her family. She was Finnish and her father was an important official in Finland. The homely twenty-one year old, able to drive and strong being a weight lifter, was given long lists of required duties: dance classes in Cranbury, music lessons at the Westminster School of Music in Princeton, recipes of beloved dishes, and housekeeping duties. Reviewed in depth with an apparently sensible young woman, Beatrice finally left after Christmas of 1984 arriving in Rome to heavy snowfall reentering her beloved other world, clutching close to her the evoked images of her family.

Bologna embraced her in a three-week snowstorm, the likes of which had not occurred for centuries, depositing mountains of velvety snow. In a carnival-like atmosphere, excited citizens filled the streets devoid of moving traffic, carving out their own footpaths to favourite shops and bars. A dramatic start to her self-imposed monastic lifestyle, necessary to accomplish two and half years of exams in the shortest possible time. By July of 1985 she had one remaining exam.

Meanwhile, Sami had become targeted by the au pair. Despite her unappealing looks and relentless increase in size he found to his horror that he was beginning to find her attractive. She was dispatched back to Finland on the first flight out on Finnish Air. The timing was apt since school was out for the summer vacation. Once again the children were packed off to England. Unfortunately for them there was another month of British school. Wearing borrowed uniforms, undergoing the ordeal of English school lunches and taunted over their American accents, they made the best of it. Daniela acquired a Liverpudlian nasal twang and gathered a bevy of adoring friends.

Beatrice picked them up to return home for a brief summer sojourn, making the best of her now emotionally distanced family. An assessment was made of the chaos and damage, willful or otherwise, inflicted by the 'highly recommended' au pair; unposted letters from Sami to her hidden under unfolded linens, unread letters lovingly written by Beatrice to the children, favourite crockery broken, a bounty of once gorgeous cashmere sweaters (gifted by her father in law each time he traveled back from London) destroyed by a wash they didn't need, cobwebs dangling from the ceiling and clumps of dust over every available surface. With the house back in order she left once more in September, took the final exam, endured a lonely graduation and worked as an intern at Sant'Orsola Hospital as she prepared for the Italian State License exam. By Christmas of '85 she was back home, after a brief detour to London to request her UK Medical License. One never knew what the future would bring.

By the end of 1985 the tide had turned for both of them. Sami was finally granted a full New York State license. He opened his own clinic on the Upper West Side forgoing large animals and affronting the long commute once again.

Beatrice started her internship at Robert Wood Johnson Hospital New Brunswick in July of 1986. Despite the brutality of long hours, she understood how fortunate she was to be working at an esteemed hospital just a 20 minute drive away. The children were now both enrolled at the local school which was conveniently just across the street. Sami bore the brunt of coordinating their care.

A telegram was sent to Jeffrey since Beatrice had not heard from him since October of 1984.

Apt. 307A Sala Daeng
77/5 Soi Sala Daeng
Silom Road
Bangkok 10500

16th February 1986

Dear Beatrice,

Just received your telegram. Sorry not to have replied to your letters. Have been settling down after a traumatic move from Paris and have been completely absorbed in my new book, which is now almost finished.

Life in Bangkok is amazing – and endless round of royal ceremonies and parties.

Robert should be in England by now with Angelica and Juan – am waiting to hear.

Congratulations on your laurea – you must be very relieved to have achieved this.

Please write soon and give me your news – I feel rather out of touch here.

With lots of love,

Jeffrey
P.S. Correspond via above address – not through Prince Piya

The pilgrimage of the young Bolivian Finestone family to the UK went splendidly. Angelica brought also her two older sons from a previous relationship. Beatrice's mother was so impressed by the obvious good upbringing of these boys that she completely revised her opinion and prejudices and took Angelica into her heart. When Beatrice eventually met Angelica herself a few years later she fully understood how her mother could not hold onto any grudges or cling to her preconceived ideas of propriety. The twelfth of thirteen children of Aymara and Quechuan descent, orphaned at an early age, brought up by her older siblings, she was an intelligent woman full of good humour and endlessly resourceful to cope with living up in the Alto Plano.

S.T. Apartment
Apt. A5
72/2 Nakorn Jaissi Road,
Sriyan, Bangkok 10300
22nd January 1987

Dear Beatrice,

Thanks for your letter – believe it or not I was about to write! having recently received your letter of last May (the one that went to N. Jersey, Bangkok, N. Jersey, La Paz, St. Annes, Bangkok!!).

Well, I'm sorry to have been so uncommunicative of late – the past year has been very unusual – settling down here, learning to read and write Siamese, but more than anything writing my book. It is now virtually complete and I am very proud of it as it has never been attempted before and the complexity of the material has been daunting – the calendar conversions (there are four) alone are bewildering. But I think I have got to grips with all the aspects. We are now getting ready for the printer and the book will be in both English and Thai, using two different calendar systems for each date!

The most recent development has been that one of the Thai royal ladies, who appears in this book, has just become engaged to the son of the Bonapartist pretender to the French throne! This is the first time ever that a dynastic marriage has occurred between a European and an Asian royal house. Admittedly the Bonapartes are not 'top drawer royals', but the pretender's mother was Princess Clementine of Belgium and his father's mother was Princess Clotilde of Savoy, daughter of King Vittorio Emanuele 11. The bridegroom descended twice from George 11, as well as from Louis Philippe 1, last Bourbon King of France, Leopald 11 of Belgium and Emperor Franz 1 of Austria. Genealogically speaking any children born of this marriage will be unique.

The wedding will be a big one in Rome, with a papal blessing at the Vatican following the service. The bride's father is an invalid, so her uncle, my old friend Prince Piya Rangsit, has been asked to give her away. I've been asked to act as his equerry! I've waited twenty years for an Asian–European royal wedding. But I never thought I'd be so closely involved with it!

I was very sorry not to be in England last summer when the whole family seemed to meet, but it just wasn't possible. But of course, I'd have loved to have seen Juan Stanley. Was sorry to hear about Aunty Betty's operation, which sounded serious. What news of your parents and of Janet?

Enclosed article on my publisher, and photos of my last birthday. Write soon. Lots of love

Jeffrey

P.S. Rushing off to a meeting in the Grand Palace.

The Foreword to Jeffrey's book, (**The Royal family of Thailand: The descendants of King Chulalongkorn**) written by Her Royal Highness Princess Galyani of Vadhana of Thailand, was full of praise for his achievement, concluding with:-

"----------for a couple of years, I have been seeing Jeffrey Finestone, dressed in the uniform required for official ceremonies, at cremations of members of the Royal Family, at gatherings of the grandchildren of King Chulalonghorn or arriving at my house with masses of papers, to exchange information about the Chakri Dynasty, from the first reign to the present reign. That is why it is a great pleasure for me to see that the book "The Royal Family of Thailand – The Descendants of King Chulalongkorn" is now being published. -----------"

The publisher also wrote a long introduction which concluded with the following statement:-

"This a major work in the field of Thai studies and is the result of sixteen years of research. It is also the first time that a full genealogy of an Asian Royal House has been published in this way."

—��—

The book was due to be published January 1989 but Jeffrey was by then in exile with a long explanation given in a letter dated 17th January 1989.

—��—

Exile: 1988-1994

10

A Christmas card, most likely for Xmas 1988, arrived with the November 4th letter of 1988 sent by circuitous route to the new address of Beatrice and Sami, highlighting the tremendous changes in both their lives and Jeffrey's on opposite sides of the world.

It had become clear by the end of her year as an intern in 1987 that the life they were grinding through in New Jersey was no longer tenable. Beatrice had an epiphany: to survive as a family they had to move to New York City where Sami had his clinic even if it meant giving up her career. But fate looked kindly upon her and Sami found for her a second-year position as a Resident in the Lower East Side at Beth Israel Hospital. Even more astounding, there was hospital housing across the street from the hospital. Despite being back in cramped quarters their life improved dramatically.

Just received your card sent to Janice in St. Annes and I notice you have a new address – enclose copy of my letter of 4th November in case it went astray, as I sent it to New Jersey!

Please write soon,
Love,
Jeffrey

To Beatrice
Seasons Greetings
And Best Wishes for
A Happy New Year

from   Jeffrey

c/o Mr. Allen Tap,
Choo ChengVhay Road
50460 Kuala Lumpur   Malaysia

4ᵗʰ, November 1988.

Dear Beatrice,

Surprise, surprise! At last a letter.
  Sorry not to have written for so long – I'm afraid that the past year has not been conducive to letter writing. In fact it is just a year since I last wrote, though I rather think that that letter never arrived, for the one I received from you in the new year seemed to imply that it hadn't.
  To put you up to date – from the beginning of the new year I was working very, very hard to finish off the book. Suddenly at the end of February everything seemed to fall in place– all the various missing dates and pieces of information and all the photographs turned up! Then something very strange happened – I got caught up in a maelstrom of events - things began to come to a head, culminate. It is far too complex to go into the whole thing – to put it briefly, there was a lot of court intrigue going on, with me at the edge of it, but suddenly I seemed to get sucked into the centre: the book was finished, after three years; then, at the end of March I trapped a nerve in my thigh and the local doctors suggested a trip to London. And so it was I left Bangkok, after performing the due

ceremonies before various statues of kings and royal deities. I had become very much involved in the rituals of court life and it has been a tremendous break.

I suddenly found myself in London – in a totally different world – a post-1984, Thatcherite, yuppie-orientated society which passes for England, - not my England, or yours. London is awful these days – nothing like the balmy days of the late 1960's and early 70's. It nearly broke my heart to see Chelsea, though, strangely, later in the summer, deep down the King's Road, I was able to find just a little of the old atmosphere (the restaurant in the Chelsea Antique Market, for instance, which is a sort of 60's time warp).

I stayed rather grandly at Lennox Gardens, Knightsbridge – as I remarked to Janice in St. Annes the corner shop was Harrods. As the summer wore on I decided to get out, and so 1ˢᵗ September I left London for Georgetown, Prince of Wales Island, the Straits Settlements — or in modern terms, Penang, Malaysia. This is a traditional place of exile for people having to leave Bangkok and the news of my arrival there created a small stir in the Siamese capital. In fact the whole thing was rather Ruritanian, with a senior member of the Thai Royal Family coming down by train to see me, and reporting back to more senior royals in Bangkok. In the 1930's, after a coup d'état, many members of the Royal Family spent a number of years in exile in Penang, which is not far from the Malayan-Thai frontier,

I decided to move from Penang to Kuala Lumpur, the capital, early last month and am visiting local publishers here. I'm thinking of doing a book on Grand Hotels of the Far East. The Thai royal book is about to be published. Have not decided whether I shall visit Bangkok for the publishing. Things are still in a state of flux, although beginning to resolve themselves. Nevertheless, the book is amazing – 500 photographs, 600 pages, texts in both English and Thai – the ultimate book on the Thai Royal Family and the first ever published genealogy of an Asian royal family: the foreward is by the King's sister. Expecting all sorts of developments once it is out.

Write me at the above address – if it sounds like China town then that is because it is – or at least, just a few streets away.

Lots of love,
Jeffrey

P.S. The doctors and specialists in London were unable to do anything about my trapped nerve – in fact they could not even diagnose it – however, I have now had four sessions with a traditional Malay masseuse and there are dramatic improvements and all goes well.

—m—

The seven years Jeffrey spent in exile, although unhappy, were immensely productive. His curiosity and exploration of South East Asian monarchy continued unabated. Proofs of a book on South East Asian Royalty were completed during this period of his life and he wrote numerous articles on non-royals who had some significance in this region. Magical descriptions of his journeys to exotic kingdoms filled his letters.

Block A. Apt 199n.
Choo Cheng Khay Apts.
Choo Cheng Khay Road,
50460 Kuala Lumpur
Malaysia

17th. January 1989

Dear Beatrice,

Many thanks for your letter – so we are back in touch at last. It was like a breath of fresh New York air hearing all your news - it brought New York back to me (as did the unexpected arrival on New Years' day of a stray Siamese cat, who has now moved in to the above address – since Harlequin I haven't had a cat, so it all came flooding back).

The book is due out in a few days' time. I enclose a xeroxed order form. I'm afraid it's the best I can manage as I am now on very bad terms with the publisher – I had hoped to be able to send you a copy, but I can't now arrange for any to be sent on my behalf – I'll be lucky if I get my own copy on time!

I say I'm in exile and I consider that I am – I had planned to remain in Thailand, so I see it in those terms. For the moment I have to wait patiently in the wings – once the book is out things will be different. The whole thing is so complicated in that I am not at the centre of it, only part of it. It revolves around my publisher, a half English, quarter Russian, Thai Princess, who looks completely European, but who is quite a senior member of the Thai Royal Family. She is now living in London, having split some while ago from her Thai boyfriend, who is the villain of the piece, and a bit of a gangster. She is now in England with her son, who is half Jewish, her husband having been a Mr. Allen Levy – they divorced after a short marriage when she met her Thai boyfriend. During the period she was living in her palace in Bangkok, which is roughly the period that I was working on the book, she got herself, and all her friends, me included, into all sorts of complicated situations. Regarding the Royal Family all is well – most of them are on my side and want me back as soon as possible, but I have been advised to wait patiently until they can see a way to getting me back – hence the publication of the book is all important. Beyond the immediate family circle, the boyfriend, her new boyfriend's family (he is English and lives in London, but is the son of a minor member of the Royal Family by an English father), there are other people involved – she managed to antagonize the Commander-in-Chief of the army this time last year! A rather sinister character, the Pravda correspondent for the whole of South-East Asia, who is based in Bangkok, is also involved in that she began leaning on him for his services as a translator (for her Russian grandmother's letters and diaries) – I steered well clear of him as long as I could, but as he was in the palace several times a week I eventually had to be polite towards him – he now accuses me of being a spy for the British government making veiled remarks about "knowing who sent me to Bangkok and why." The whole thing is almost unbelievable – however, I know I have the family behind me, including the King's sister, so all I can do is wait.

It's probably not half as dramatic as it sounds – it's just typically Asian! And over here these things have a way of sorting themselves out, especially if you know the right people, which of course I do. I am in constant communication with all sorts of people in Bangkok, from the King's sister down – Prince Piya Rangsit came down to see me not long ago – and I know they are working on something at the moment to effect my return. Mind you, I always wanted a Ruritanian lifestyle and now I've got one!

Last week I had a visit from Anthony and Marie-Christine (cousin Freda's son and daughter-in-law), who were on a tour of the Far East and we spent a very pleasant couple of days together. They spoke of you and I told them the story of the time you had tea with Hitler (or was it drinks with General Amin?) and they were very amused.

Regarding my trapped nerve – I call it that, as the doctors in London didn't want to call it anything. I got it by sitting, over a period of time, in a wicker chair without a cushion. There was no pain but my legs went stiff for a few days. Now, with the massage, it seems to have been cured.

Will keep you informed as to developments. Write soon.

Lots of love Jeffrey

Kuala Lumpur, 19ᵗʰ August 1989

Dear Beatrice,

Many thanks for your two letters. Its ages since I heard from you and I wonder whether a letter got lost – did you reply to mine of 17ᵗʰ January?

So glad that you like the book and are duly impressed.

Was amazed to hear about Ramon and Jackie's visit – extraordinary. However did you manage to keep in touch?

Many thanks for the article on the Sultan of Brunei - quite well written.

So now we are in the same line of business – both studying genetics!

Was equally horrified by your account of your visit to a baseball game (base obviously being the operative word) – I think I'd have reacted the same way. I understand your reaction completely - I think an over sensibility to the cruder aspects of modern life is a Beacon inheritence! The Thai would say you are very "paddy" about the game – standoffish in an aristocratic well-bred fashion – usually used as a compliment.

I have moved to a new flat – in the same block – so my address is now:-

Block A, Apt. 197R.

For the moment I am staying put in Malaysia – but things could change depending on the circumstances and it is very difficult at the moment to make any plans – so I can't say when or where we could meet and I don't think a visit to Asia would be worth planning in case I suddenly move. I'm working hard on my Malay royal genealogies and might be doing a book, but everything is very much up in the air at the present time.

Was amused by Daniela knowing what your parents would be doing in Churston Road by the hour of the day!

Please watch out for any other interesting articles – I can't always get things out here (although I make up for it with items of local interest of course!)

Often miss New York, especially when I see some films, such as "Working Girl" or "Ghostbusters 11". But I can't see myself returning to America – I think it was a phase of my life.

Write soon.
Lots of love
Jeffrey

———ɯ——

After completing her three years of Residency there were more family tensions looming up. Sami could not decide where to move now that the hospital housing would no longer be available. He yearned to return to country life. But the children had been heroic in putting up with all the changes of countries, states, schools and homes. They had finally been enrolled in the UN school, which was walking distance from the hospital residence. Any discussion of moving became a huge source of contention. And then a miracle happened. Beatrice was offered a Fellowship in Genetics at the same hospital, granting a two-year reprieve on decision making. They could continue to stay on in their small but adequate apartment.

During this transition from Residency to Fellowship, Jackie and Ramon came to visit, bringing Jackie's now grownup daughters. Ramon appeared fatigued and at the end of the visit gave them the sobering news that he had just been diagnosed with Multiple Sclerosis. As vivacious as ever, Jackie with her halo of red hair, glowed with delight at being able to present her children to them. Her maternal rights had been abolished when she had moved in with Ramon so many years ago. She was 10 years older than Ramon and since he was just 16 years old when they started their 'illicit affair' she had been deemed an unsuitable mother. She was not allowed to receive her daughters until she actually married Ramon.

—∞—

Kuala Lumpur, 16th October 1989

Dear Beatrice,

Many thanks for your letter and card – was delighted to hear from Ramon and Jackie and what memories their card of the beach at Brighton brought!! By the way, you are still using my old address. I am now in apartment 197R (not 199D). Otherwise the address is exactly the same.

Can you please send me Ramon and Jackie's address and I shall write to them.

Might be starting a new book - -on the royalty of South-East Asia in old photographs – rather like "The Last Courts of Europe". A nice easy book after the endless research for the Thai book in which I ended up reading and writing Siamese!

How are your parents – I often think of them and wonder how they are getting on. Please pass my love to them.

The Queen and Prince Philip are at present in Malaysia on a state visit prior to next week's Commonwealth Prime Ministers Conference. Saw them arriving at the state banquet two days ago. A fortnight back I went down to the Palace of the Sultan of Selengor, about twenty miles from K.L, and there was a rehearsal for the Queen's tea party given by the Sultan (on the day she actually arrived). We rehearsed for a while then ate the tea- all very nice.

Please send any interesting news cuttings when you can – I don't see the English press here.

Write soon, Lots of love,
Jeffrey.

Block A, Flat 197R.
Choo Cheng Khay Apts.,
50460 Kuala Lumpur.

3rd December 1989.

Dear Beatrice,

Many thanks for your letter and for Ramon and Jackie's address.

Made two trips during November – Trengannu on the east coast of Malaysia. Had tea with the Sultan's wife, who I last met in 1982 – she has my last book and was very excited to see the new one. Stayed about ten days, attended a royal wedding in the palace and interviewed numerous royals for my Trengganu family tree. Then a week later I flew to Sumatra – my first ever visit. It was absolutely fascinating – very different from Peninsular Malaya, which I had expected it to resemble. Stayed in Medan. One of the big differences is in the architecture – whereas everything old in Malaysia is English, in Indonesia, everything old is Dutch! The purpose of the visit was to meet the Royal Family of Deli – the Sultanate was officially abolished in 1946, but as is so often the case the Royal family still live in the palace (a marvelous Victorian Moorish extravaganza) – I got chased around the Moorish throne room in the dark one night by a gay prince!

Was back in New York last week when I went to see the new (or perhaps not so new) Bette Midler film, most of which is set in the Plaza. It was extremely funny.

Next month it will be twenty years since I fled from Liverpool into exile in London. What a cuffuffle that all was!

Have a marvelous Christmas and New Year,

Lots of love,
Jeffrey.

Postcard April 4th 1990 (from Bangkok)

Bangkok, 10.4.90

Here for a few days for the funeral of Prince Piya Rangsit, my old friend, Amazing to be back after so long.

Love,
Jeffrey.

K.L., 11ᵗʰ May 1990

Dear Beatrice,

Many thanks for card – it arrived on my birthday!
I'm paying a quick visit to England from 23ʳᵈ May to
do photo research on my new book (a sort of Asian version
of "The Last Courts of Europe").

Robert is planning to come over to see me – we haven't
met for almost seven years.
Bangkok was as amazing as ever, as ever.

Will write more fully when I return to K.L.
Lots of love,
Jeffrey.

———〰———

Inspired by Janice Finestone's photo presentation of La Paz back in 1984, Beatrice took the children to Bolivia the summer of 1990. Sami was unable to join them, since he could not leave his clinic.

Robert and Angelica had moved up from La Paz to the Altiplano where the city of El Alto was expanding rapidly.

Always lightheaded from the thinly oxygenated air, everything was experienced with a heightened clarity of senses.

Robert had created a walled domain with ample living quarters built of mud bricks. Angelica had her own wing on the ground level where she conducted her business. Robert applied his gardening skills in the expansive greenhouse built of clear plastic with raised vegetable beds providing much needed greens especially during the winter months. A large chicken coup also flanked one of the walls of the ample grounds. A central rectangular area masqueraded as a lawn, sprouting coarse sparse grass. A number of dogs roamed this diminutive estate, essential for protection.

Angelica oversaw the knitting of wool sweaters, a complex process involving the receiving of wool pelts from far distant sheep farms; the distribution to a number of local women for spinning on spindles carried by hand; sending the spun wool back down to La Paz for dying with vegetable dyes; wool skeins of various muted colours were then sent back up to the Finestone domain. There Angelica would hold court on a weekly basis, doling out the skeins which had been carefully weighed, details handwritten into a ledger in her office. In exchange she received the knitted sweaters from the previous week's assignment. Business concluded the ladies, wearing bowler hats, bodies encased in voluminous colorful skirts, warm shawls draped over their shoulders, hands busy spinning yarn, would sit in a circle on the lawn and exchange stories. A stern leader, Angelica would have already decided who to dismiss from this group of workers if deemed unable to adhere to the high standard demanded in their work. Daniela was concerned for those who had lost their job but Angelica had no qualms: "they can always go back to the market and sell their vegetables" was her taut reply.

Robert kept himself busy teaching Bolivians about his greenhouses and giving private English lessons, eventually opening up his own English Language School called the 'Speak Easy Institute.'

To the utter disbelief of his parents he had given up a Fellowship at Caius College in Cambridge where he had received a First Class Honours Degree in Politics, Philosophy and Economics. It was incomprehensible to them that anyone would turn their back on such an offer for a privileged life. He described himself as an anarchist. The two brothers were poles apart in their belief systems.

Nonetheless, Robert took good care of his guests, hiring extra help for washing clothes, done by hand in the yard, and helping the "godmother," his euphemism for the servant, with shopping and cooking.

Daniela and Gabriele coped with the inconveniences, the most notable being the outdoor latrine which at night was negotiated by candlelight. There was no door to close for privacy and to their utmost disbelief the hole was flushed by a bucket of water filled from a pump in the yard.

—m—

Kuala Lumpur, 12ᵗʰ December 1990
To Beatrice, Sami, Daniela, and Gabriele

Wishing you a Very Merry Christmas and New Year

Many thanks for letter – it arrived whilst I was away in
Java at a royal Wedding (enclosed a pic of me with one of
the palace dance-troupe).
    Thanks for the lovely photo of your trip to La Paz – it
was lovely seeing you all together or as an American lady
at Robert's wedding said "ipso facto you guys", a delightful
combination American slang and Latin!
    Can't say yet about coming next December – will not
be able to decide till nearer the time.

Lots of love,
Jeffrey

P.S. Also enclosed my article on W. Somerset Maugham.

The article on Somerset Maugham, published by Malaysian
Tatler November 1990, was a fitting tribute to one of the greatest
writers in the English language. Somerset Maugham fell under the
spell of the Far East during his first visit to Malay during the 1920's,
his last visit taking place in 1960. Jeffrey evokes the atmosphere of
the town, undoubtedly Malacca, which provided Maugham with so
much material for his writing.

Beatrice was in the throes of preparing for Gabriele's barmitzvah
the following year. She had alerted her cousin to the date of this
event.

K.L., 26th April 1991.

Dear Beatrice,

Its' ages since I've written- was spurred into writing at the heartrending news that the Plaza Hotel is turning into flats! I recently heard a reading of "The Great Gatsby" on the Overseas Service with that marvelous scene in a suite at the Plaza in the 1920's. The suite is high up overlooking the Park in the middle of a heatwave and all the doors and windows are flung open wide — way, way down on the ground floor a wedding reception is in progress and the music from the ballroom wafts up to the suite floors and floors above. I have memories of the Hotel Majestic, St. Annes, which move me in the same way — my enduring passion for certain grand hotels took root in the Majestic at a very early age. One of my earliest memories is of being a child 'mannequin' in a fashion show — I must have been three or four — I had to walk out on a long catwalk leading from the stage out across the ballroom floor (I wore a little 'Prince Charles coat' with a velvet collar). And what vivid recollections you still have of my barmitzvah luncheon in the same room? A very few I should imagine — but you did stay at the Majestic for that three day event — everyone did, even Uncle Henry, Aunt Edie, Hilary and John. And Robin made a sudden appearance from Sussex — until I was introduced to him I'd never even known he existed (he "wasn't spoken of") and Stevie, his younger half brother, was naughty on the Pier. There was endless trouble with the 'Koshros committee' because I insisted on having the lunch on the Saturday, rather than the following day — and even though the Majestic had a 'kosher kitchen' with two sets of plates, and we agreed to having cold fresh salmon which didn't need to be re-cooked instead of hot roast chicken, which had been my choice, Reverend and Mrs. Feldinger were persuaded by the 'koshros committee' to boycott the meal and in fact did not attend! A special Italian dessert covered in spun sugar had been "created" by the foreign chef — I came across similar desserts years later in the dining room of the Hôtel de Paris at Monte Carlo! It was all a great success despite having assumed a certain notoriety by the boycotting by the Rev, and Mrs. Feldinger. Looking back on it it now seems grander than some royal weddings I've been to.

Which gets me neatly round to the subject of another family barmitzvah. As things are I don't see myself being able to come – things have not been so good financially after the Thai book and I am busy trying to get something new out in K.L., which is nearing completion – a sort of "Last Courts of Asia"- something of a sequel to "The Last Courts of Europe" on all the Royal Families of South-East Asia; much more exuberant visually; plus, of course, a chapter on Siam. It's a pity you have never been to the Far East – perhaps you'll come and see me when you've recovered from the barmitzvah. There are good round trips from the West Coast, and presumably starting in New York, which would cover all popular destinations – Bangkok, Penang and Singapore. Funny thing, but that's how I got here ten years ago, from New York, via San Francisco, Honolulu, Tokyo, Kyoto, Hong Kong and Macao! Then I flew from Hong Kong to Singapore and checked myself into the Raffles (the only possible thing to do), then crossed into Malaya (Malaysia) and eventually ended up in Bangkok in time for the bicentenary of the Chakri Dynasty in April 1982. This time ten years ago you were living in the Catskills and possibly Harlequin wasn't even born. Beatrice, I'll never forget that crazy party on Long Island, and Cynthia, and Yoko in the next village, and the champagne, which was reluctant to start flowing but when it did it never stopped and the weird little vegetables carved into peculiar shapes – remember those? – and the Hockney and the torture chamber in the Attic and the loudspeakers on the beach. That was quite a party!

Of course, I shall want to hear all about the affair both before and after – I'll want to know details like "who is doing the catering?" and whether you have to go downtown to a meeting of the "Koshros committee on the Lower East Side, that sort of thing.

How are your parents? – although I spoke to them on the phone last summer I didn't really get told any news. I hear from cousin Janice in St. Annes about Aunty Betty, but in her last letter she said that she hadn't heard any news for a long time and was going to phone Freda.

And what news of Ramon and Jackie?

Please keep on sending me the odd interesting cutting – but don't send too large an envelope as I have trouble with anything that doesn't fit into the small slit – better to stuff an airmail size envelope than using a bigger, commercial envelope. Most of my mail goes to an office in town, really all except yours and Robert's and a royal in Bangkok.

Please write soon and get me up to date on what's going on family-wise.

Lots of love,
Jeffrey.

How evocative was this letter full of nostalgia.

Beatrice laughed about the description of The Party. She had actually forgotten about the 'chamber'. The night they had slept with the Andy Warhols, Jeffrey had noticed a ladder leading up to a small door high up in the rafters. Having a fear of heights Beatrice declined to follow Jeffrey, as he scrambled up full of curiosity to see what lay behind the door. As he pushed it open he gasped – it was a small chamber full of whips and handcuffs and other nefarious looking instruments. He ventured no further. They had speculated over the various possible scenes and then promptly fell asleep. It had been a long day.

27.9.1991 POSTCARD
from:Pahang Malaysia

Thanks for letter and most interesting Russian article.
Glad you found a new apt.
I'm in a hill station for a few days – to cool off.

Love,
Jeffrey.

The Fellowship completed, Sami and Beatrice had moved to the Upper West Side renting an apartment as they continued to battle over where they should live. Sami still wanted to move out of the city. Admittedly, the early 90's were abysmal. Every wall and flat surface was covered with graffiti; crack vials lined every nook and cranny and carpeted the pavements; the homeless hung out on street corners often menacing with flailing arms and staggering steps of the unhinged; Aids victims unfortunate enough to contract the illness before the advent of sophisticated anti-viral therapy reminded one daily of death as they shuffled emaciated along the littered streets; and stray bullets were flying aimlessly from trigger happy criminals and police alike. Of course Beatrice understood all that, but at that point in their lives another move for the children was out of the question.

In the meantime, plans continued for the big event.

The barmitzvah went well. A banquet of delicious Iraqui food, kosher of course, was served and Jeffrey would have approved. The synagogue, housed in a former Quaker Meeting House built in 1859, was not as sumptuous as the grand victorian Majestic Hotel of St. Annes on Sea but the Quaker aesthetics of balance and harmony made up for that. Above all, Jeffrey would have appreciated the serendipity of life. Beatrice had joined the local synagogue and discovered to her astonishment that the rabbi who had been reluctant to marry them so many years earlier had relocated and established a significant and successful congregation in Gramercy Park. Rabbi Bloch was delighted to officiate at the barmitzvah of the son of a couple he had married so many years before. Furthermore, both sets of grandparents were present. His original misgivings were atoned.

POSTCARD

Pontianak Borneo – 16.11.91

Thanks for the invitation – much regret but unable to attend as in the depths of Borneo!
Hope all goes well.

Lots of love,
Jeffrey.

P.S. Very impressed that it is to be at Gramercy Park! So posh!

Xmas Card 12/91
Greetings of the Season
and a joyous New Year

To Beatrice, Sami, Daniela and Gabriele

Thanks for letter
you forgot to include Michael's address
please send so I can write

Forgot all about the great date then on that Saturday morning I woke with a dream I was in New York – actually there!

How about that?
from Jeffrey

At the back of the envelope was written :-

Thanks for the article on my old friend Charlie Amatyakul. Loved all that fuss in the Plaza's kitchens in the preparation for Queen Sirikit's banquet for 250 – just who did the catering! – perhaps they should have used the "kosher committee". God bless the Plaza (- and the Majestic, St. Annes)

POSTCARD

Penjengat, 21.1.1992

Thanks for Michael's address. Am here with the heir to the throne of Riau who joined me in Singapore and who is my guide. Longing to see some photos of the big event!

Love,
Jeffrey

[Penyengot Island, Indonesia, was the seat of the Malay Kingdom and is famous for its viceroys of Riau during the eighteenth century.]

A card dated 1992 arrived depicting *"street decorations, Bangkok, to mark Queen Sirikit's 60th birthday August – 1992 (just like the Illuminations!)."*

Jeffrey's comment alludes to the famous annual Illuminations of Blackpool, near to St.Annes, displayed at the end of summer. These fantastical displays had originally celebrated the Royals first visit to Blackpool in 1912. Aunt Freda had diligently taken Beatrice every year to view the lights from the top deck of a bus. The event always seemed to take place when it was raining. Through low dark grey clouds, the haze of the illuminations produced a surreal visionary world of phantasms.

POSTCARD

Bangkok, 9th August 1992.

Greetings from Bangkok and Queen Sirikit's 60th birthday celebrations.
Any word from the New York bookshops? The book's cover is now designed and will go to the Frankfort Book Fair in October.

Love,
Jeffrey

The letter pertaining to NY bookshops must not have arrived, since Beatrice had no recollection of it. Presumably he was referring to his work 'South East Asian Royalty.' Maybe it was lost during their move to yet another apartment. Sami had finally agreed to stay in New York and peace reigned. Their teenage children put up with the move, without too much enthusiasm, into an apartment which required an immense amount of work to be restored to its former 'prewar' glory. But it was to be their definitive home and Beatrice threw all her hopes into creating a welcoming anchor for the future.

It was after his visit to the Frankfurt Book Fair that Jeffrey put Beatrice in touch with a publishing agent on the Upper West Side to discuss his new work. An impressive flyer and an article on the new book, printed in "Malaysia Tatler" May 1993, was sent for her perusal. After contacting the agent she was invited to her home. An elegant refined lady of a certain age greeted Beatrice warmly. Having met Jeffrey at the Book Fair she spoke highly of him and his work but regretted not being able to help since royal topics were not her specialty.

—𝔪—

POSTCARD

4ᵗʰ July 1993
Phnom Penh, Cambodia

Having a lovely time wish you were here.

Love
Jeffrey

With tongue in cheek Jeffrey sent the standard English postcard wishes. Unfortunately, it was more or less the last whimsical joke uttered by him.

Beatrice had started to call her cousin by phone. She discerned that on his return from Cambodia, the summer of 1993, he was violently ill. A haunting conversation, ensued during this particular call, revealed that he was in the throes of a debilitating attack of dysentery. He had not a soul to take care of him. Dazed she had put down the receiver, echoes of his weak voice reverberating in her head, only to call him back minutes later. She feared he was moribund. Jeffrey was so proud that he had to be at death's door to admit his impecunious situation. He agreed to accept some money but had no bank account. He balked at the idea of sending cash. "It would be stolen believe me" was his barely audible response, voice quavering. Inquiries revealed that even money orders could not be cashed in Malaysia leaving little choice. After discussing the situation with Sami they decided to go through the British Embassy. It was late

Friday evening when they disturbed the British Consulate General on duty in New York. He seemed quite buoyant about the matter, probably thinking a large quantity of dollars were to be exchanged, since they later discovered that at the other end a twenty-five per cent cut was made. "Oh goodness, I know the old chap in Kuala Lumpur, a jolly good lad he is. We attended the same school, you know. He is just taking up duties there." He was referring to the British Consulate General, his counterpart in Kuala Lumpur. "Yes," he concluded "I'll be very happy to facilitate you."

Early Saturday morning, Sami presented himself at the Consulate, cash in hand, and was reassured that Jeffrey would receive the money personally.

The following week Beatrice called to ensure all was well, that her cousin was recovering and that he had received the appropriate amount of cash. She was violently assaulted verbally. Apparently her cousin had felt humiliated at the British Embassy and to add insult to injury, she had been informed that it was actually King Bedouin of Belgium who had 'saved' him. After departing from the Embassy, he had taken himself to a café for sustenance and read about the King's demise in the newspaper. Somehow he saw this as a sacrifice on behalf of the King thus saving Jeffrey's life! - hallucination or sly humour? She was just happy he was well enough to be so irate.

This barrage of anger was followed by a long letter written in two parts:-

1

Visit to the British High Commission, Kuala Lumpur, Thursday 5th August 1993

For almost five years since leaving Bangkok I have for various reasons avoided all contact with the British High Commission in Kuala Lumpur, partly for reasons explained on the telephone but more particularly for reasons associated with my personal assumption of Thai nationality and allegiances made during my stay in Bangkok in the 1980's.

However, circumstances dictated that I should visit the High Commission, and below is a strictly personalized account of what happened.

I went early in the morning to ensure that what little physical strength I had would suffice for the duration of the visit. Mr. Campbell had instructed the security guards that I would be arriving but I still had to undergo the usual stringent security procedure administered by the Indian security staff employed by the High Commission in order to enter the premises.

I entered the consular waiting room which was full of about one hundred and fifty nig-nogs (local people wishing to apply for visa entries to the mother country – Great Britain- for purpose of study – these for the most part were Chinamen and women with the obligatory sprinkling of Indians and other races which form 10% of the population of this God-forsaken country – the master-race, the Malays, wishing to study in Great Britain do not apply in person to the High Commission for an entry visa but receive it through applications made by the Malaysian Government direct to the High Commission). As a member of the former master race (i.e. the British), I made my way past four windows designated for Malaysian citizens to the fifth window marked British subjects. I could feel the eyes of the one hundred and fifty local nig-nogs on me as I crossed the floor – to reach the fifth window I had to pass a charming portrait in oils of the Queen painted in 1977 (one I had not seen before) and in the Thai way presented my respects by "wei-ing' it with clasped hands – goodness knows what the nig-nogs made of that! My attitude to local people is complex – on some occasions I see them in terms of the British historical background of this country, formerly Malaya, and now a non-democratic fundamentalist

Islamic state with strong anti-British anti-Western and in particular antisemitic policies (the Jewish community in Penang Island left for Singapore a number of years ago); but on most occasions I see them from purely Siamese (Thai) point of view – whatever their race, be it Malay, Chinese or Indian, they are considered in all ways inferior to the Thai race (this belief has become intensified of late by the lack of respect Malaysians have shown to their royalty – such behaviour being seen as beneath contempt by the Thais who revere their monarch in a way to be found in no other country in the world. So from either of these of these two viewpoints I hold the population in very low esteem).

At the window for the former master-race I requested to see Mr. Campbell and was quickly shown into a private waiting room. By this time my emotions were running high but fortunately was able to compose myself in the two minutes before he came into the room. Poor man, he'd only been in the country 12 days! He seemed ruffled by the small amount of money in the envelope as I think I mentioned on the phone – I had brought with me the proofs of two chapters of the book, the Thai and Malaysian chapter, which I let him look at and despite my feeble physical state ensured that the 10-15 minute meeting was conducted along correct diplomatic lines with 'small talk' about all number of things, rather as a meeting between two ambassadors during a period of crisis, skirting the actual issues other than when entirely necessary and sparing us both any further emotional strain. His concern was human and genuine enough and he asked only that when I return to Thailand that I inform the High Commission of my doing so. He advised that I eat plenty of eggs in order to build up my strength which advice I gracefully accepted. Then I was out through the door and past the 150 waiting nig-nogs and out onto the street. A more embarrassing and humiliating meeting I cannot recall.

11

Proposed amendment to the oral Beacon traditions restricted to all Beacons, their descendants both in the male and female lines, inclusive of legal spouses as in use since the year 1976 and stating that "Peking killed Uncle Arthur" - it is hereby proposed that the additional words be added to the 1976 dictum to read as follows:-

"Peking killed Uncle Arthur but His late majesty King Baudouin 1 of the Belgians saved Jeffrey".

* Note that the old spelling of Peking, not Beijing, is used and that the pronunciation according to Beacon usage is more correctly Peeking with the emphasis on the first consonant.

Amusing, even when in dire straits, that Jeffrey could not resist dredging up the Beacon myths. Uncle Arthur had passed away not long after that trip to The Far East and at subsequent family gatherings one would often hear in the background of cheery chatter "Peking did him in you know."

K.L., August 31ˢᵗ 1993

Dear Beatrice and Sami,

One month later!
Well, I seem to have made an adequate recovery – sorry about all the bru-ha-ha and hope that my account of my visit to the British High Commission was not too cryptic or too bizarre for you (by August 12ᵗʰ I was back in the Thai Embassy to sign the book of congratulations for

Queen Sirikit's birthday – I had defected again!). Colin Campbell's nig-nog secretary sent me a form to fill in, in case of a local emergency (revolution, civil war, that sort of thing) so that they would know who and where I was – as it is so thick the envelope I thought that it was an invitation and that maybe Princess Margaret or the Gloucesters were coming over and that I was invited to the reception – I was so disgusted when I opened the envelope that I immediately tore it up!

The book is now almost printed and should be out before too long.

I am now beginning to think of my return to Bangkok – tomorrow will be the fifth anniversary of me arriving in Malaysia from London and it is high time that I returned to Thailand. Was very upset to learn that the anti-royal feeling in Malaysia is as strong as ever – the Sultan of Pahang (who was King of Malaysia from 1979 to 1984) arrived in Brussels to represent the country and the King at King Baudouin's funeral and the Malaysian Embassy in Brussels informed him that he would have to pay for the hotel himself and his retinue – quite sickening – imagine if the Thai Embassy had informed the Crown Prince of such a thing on his arrival!! The sooner I leave this country for good the better and once my book is out I shall be persona non grata anyway!

I've stopped the chicken soup - it having served its purpose – however, I've now got into chopped liver and make a mean serving with the obligatory grated egg on top.

Lots of love,
Jeffrey

Her cousin was back to his teasing once more, thank goodness, but Beatrice wondered if she would ever be truly forgiven for her perceived transgressions.

K.L. 25ʰ Oct.1993

Dear Beatrice, Thanks for your letter and cutting,

I'm afraid I too was a bit precipitous – the party is now not going to be in December, but possibly March. Had a marvelous five days in Bangkok but the outcome was a change in plans, to accommodate the inclusion of Princess Galyani Vadhana in things. We had a meeting with the Thai book distributors who distributed my Thai book in Bangkok and at least from them, among other things, that when Michael Jackson was in Bangkok two months ago he visited their main shop and bought only one thing: a recently published book of photographs of King Chulalongkorn! My canny Malaysian publisher said we'd better send him a leaflet for the new book and I said, what about Elizabeth Taylor? And he replied, yes, her also.

Meanwhile the book is about to be printed and bound and I'm preparing to return to Bangkok to live.

I know you'll get to see Bangkok one day and by then I'll be reinstalled there.

Lots of love,
Jeffrey.

Vague plans to visit Thailand with the family were being discussed for some future date so Beatrice was pleased to note that they would be welcomed.

The Return to Bangkok 1994-1997

25ᵗʰ July 1994.

S.T. Apartments,
72/2 Nakorn Jaisri Rd.,
Sriyan,
10300 Bangkok.

Tel. 243.1107

Dear Beatrice,

Sorry not to have written for so long – I've just completed my move back to Bangkok – it took three months and two trips up and down – the seven trunks went by sea, down the Peninsula then up into the Gulf of Siam – full of books.

Happy to be back – I've even taken my old flat! And they've given me the 1986 rent back! (without raising it).

I'm on satellite T.V. (since ten days) – B.B.C. (of course). Music channel from Hong Kong and Star T.V., which is no good. I can also get Rangoon (Burma), which is good for a laugh, but a little goes a long way – I asked if I could change to the Royalist FUNCINPEC channel in Phnon-Penh but, much to my disappointment, they said no. So I am stuck with Rangoon Maybe I'll send in a request in for "On the Road to Mandalay"!

The book seems to have sunk without trace. Things went from bad to worse in Malaysia. On top of last year's so called "Royalty Crisis," this year there has been a wave of anti-British feeling, engineered by the government, over the Perggau Dam affair and the Sunday Times freedom to write about it without Mr. Major's hindering them – the Malaysian govt. couldn't understand this, took deep umbrage, and called off all intergovernmental business deals. With Britain!! And three months after the King and Queen had paid the first state visit to London since 1974! Things became more and more Islamic and anti-Western by the day – and the anti-royal attitude is firmly entrenched with government approval. It's such a relief to be back in Siam and to be able to stand for the Royal Anthem before each cinema performance!

Write soon.
Lots of love,
Jeffrey.

—⟋⟍—

Bangkok, 3ʳᵈ September 2537*

Dear Beatrice,

Thanks for your letter – sorry I wasn't "in" to receive your phone call. Actually I was in bed as the call came during the early hours of the morning (5am) I didn't pick up. Suggest you phone the office of the Permanent Thai Mission to the

U.N. in N.Y. to check the exact time difference. Best time to phone between 11.00 a.m. and 1.00 p.m. and between 5.00 p.m. and 9.00 p.m.

Settling in nicely to my Bangkok life. Yesterday, I met, for the first time in 29 years, my old classmate from Whittinghame College – the family own a bank so it can't do any harm to keep in touch! Needless to say we split several atoms and it was gratifying to hear from him that he always thought how 'cute' I looked at school– not that he ever mentioned it at the time and spent all his free hours at the notorious Sombrero Club in Hove, haunt of au-pair girls and exchange students. Still, it was nice to know after all this time and did my ego good. He was the only boy at Whittinghame College who the masters addressed by his nickname as his surname (granted to the family by King Vajiravudh in 1916) was too much for them! I kept putting off contacting him last time I was here as I concentrated myself entirely on the book and my social life was strictly limited to people in the book.

Yes, do plan a trip to Bangkok in 2 or 3 years, provided I haven't become a monk or something.

Lots of love,
Jeffrey

*1994: The solar calendar was adapted by King Chulalongkorn in 1888 and is the official calendar. However, the Thai lunar calendar continues in use.]

Beatrice was taken aback by an invite for two or three years hence. Why not earlier? That question was soon answered.

—〰—

S.T. Apartments
72/Nakorn Jaisri Road,
Sriyan,
Bangkok 10300.

23rd November 1994/2537

Dear Beatrice,

Thanks for your letter and cuttings.

I'm replying quickly to let you know that early next year is not going to be good for me if you were to come over. Although I've settled in, in one sense, in that I've returned to my old flat and resumed my old activities, in another way I'm not properly settled, due to the inordinate amount of time I spent away – six and half years- and certain problems concerning the ongoing battle with the publisher of my first Thai book. On top of that I'm due to begin my new book in January and will be very busy for the rest of the year. It's going to be a relative quickie, by popular demand (or should I say royal command) for a book on the family of King Mongkut (Rama 1V) – it will be published for the forthcoming golden jubilee of the King and I'm going to have to move quick once things get under way. At the moment I'm preparing three specimen chapters for my new publisher, Lady Priya (daughter of my old friend Prince Piya Rangsit) to show around. She seems to want to outdo the first Thai book, and publish my sequel. As she said in conversation "if I can build a condo I can publish a book" (she's building an immense condo now - 34 stories – on land which a bitchy friend described as "not quite prime"- but near enough as damn it!). She used to be married to the son of the Maharaja of Jaipur (the only time the Queen has ever spoken to me was at her wedding reception in Cadogan Place!) and is now married to a former Thai heart-throb who still occasionally records popular songs in the Thai language.

So I'm gearing up to begin on a new book – meanwhile in K.L. there are languorous moves to bring out "The Royal Families of South-East Asia" – they're supposed to have a launch in the new year and I suppose I shall have to go down for it, albeit reluctantly. The new King and Queen are supposed to be the guests of honour, but I'll believe it when it happens.

So I'm keeping my fingers crossed that all goes well this time. I had said that I wasn't going to do another book, but it seems that I'm going to have to.

I was amazed to learn that I have a cousin who is a Lubavitcher! I only ever heard of the movement once I was well grown up and it began hitting the news - Nothing was ever said at Whittinghame College in the ten years that I was there. By the way, I suggest you look under Thailand in the new Whittinghame College old boys guide and you will see two people listed, myself and my old classmate, who I have now twice seen for lunch.

By the way Lady Priya. is toying with the idea of doing a Thai publication of the K.L. book once it is out in Malaysia – this of course would involve a party, as well later of the possibility of a launching party for the new Thai book, as it might be better to wait for either of these events for you to visit here. Then I could probably get you put up at the Oriental for free.

Lots of love
Jeffrey.

Beatrice wondered whether or not Jeffrey was referring to the Queen of England or Queen of Thailand who spoke to him at the reception in Cadogan Place. Since the exchange took place in London, she presumed it was the former.

—⚬—

Bangkok, 5th November 1995.

Dear Beatrice,

Many thanks for your letters of 24th August and 26th Oct. Sorry not to have written sooner.

Things have not been easy of late – I'm living in some hardship, yet again, though have managed to complete writing my new book in just seven months, but once again I'm caught in a poverty trap. The book cannot be published for the meanwhile – the setting up of a new publishing company, the design itself and the prolonged period of court mourning following the death of the King's mother, the Princess Mother, last July, precluded us from being able to publish before the state funeral (cremation) – i.e. after March at the earliest. Meanwhile my Malaysian masterpiece has disappeared without trace and so, although I am securely back in Thailand and I have been working hard all year, I have nothing to show for it and my life is in the doldrums. As a result my health is suffering. Also, the long years of exile (six and a half) have meant that I have lost out completely on any reflected glory over the publication of the immense Thai royal book after my departure in 1988. Apart from the inner circle of the present royal family (who themselves know well enough what I did and pay me all due honour and credit for it, in private) I am virtually unknown to the Thai public and I find that a bitter pill to swallow. Also, there will almost certainly be more trouble from the first publisher who, I'm pretty sure, will attempt to prevent having the new book published – it remains to be seen what will happen, but think now I shall just have to fight her when the time comes.

I heard from Freda her own tragic family news and tried to relate to it, but with difficulty – our circumstances are so very different – when she is hit by tragedy she is sheltered from it by the bosom of a lovely family and ample wealth to weather the tumult – the tragedy of my last eight years weigh heavy and it is a burden which I have become used to bearing alone.

You're the only one who still seems to write! Can't get a reply from Robert, nor from Janice in St.Annes, who is now committed to some Balkan relief operation (I can't even work out which side she's supposed to be on!)* However, apart from family I do have a number of other correspondents, either obscure royalty scattered around the world, or royalty obsessed commoners. Sorry to sound so negative – perhaps things will improve soon.

Lots of love
Jeffrey.

* Like Bismark, when asked if he knew the answer to the "Schleswig-Holstein Question, "I would reply that yes, I did once know, but had now forgotten what it was as it was too complicated to remember!". Uncle Peter used to like that particular quote!

26ᵗʰ November

Dear Beatrice,

Many thanks for your letter and for the $20 – I'm glad you didn't send more as its very risky.

My problem is that I've had a very bad year financially with two major works (books) going down the drain. As with successful business venture, profit making, the results are cumulative (like interest) – so with poverty, the effect long term is also cumulative. When I left Malaysia to return to Thailand I'd made some money from letting the Malaysian National Archives have some of my Malay papers and this enabled my return to Bangkok (a very expensive business as I had to import my entire South East Asian and Thai collection of books and papers from Kuala Lumpur).

Now, 18 months later, despite just finishing writing yet another Asian book, the third, I don't see things improving and I am back in the poverty trap. You ask what I think you should do. The only thing that occurs to me (and I already thought of it before) is to seek assistance from the Whittinghame Club, which is composed of some extremely rich members. But it is very difficult to actually write such a letter to the old assistant headmaster, who I've been in correspondence with since you put me in touch with them a couple of years ago. Another old Whittinghame author, Eric Shane, seems to have done very well from his art books.

Tell me what you and Sami think of approaching the old boys Club. Perhaps it could be done through some of the New York members, rather than me having to write myself to broach the matter. I have the school's latest address list with telephone number, which I could send you.

Although the new book is finished the printing and publishing of it are going to take quite a long time and even then it probably won't turn out to be a money spinner the Malaysian book was meant to have been (remember all that flurry about Frankfurt – it seems a 100 years ago now and its only just two!) Also, I suspect that my first publisher might try to take out an injunction to try to prevent its publication (because of an obscure clause in my contract with her – it's just 10 years since that contract was signed in November 1985 – which makes mention of any book on King Mongkut's family, which is what I have just completed for Priya, going to her company for publication) – if she wants to cause trouble then she could.

Many thanks for your concern, which I appreciate.

Love,
Jeffrey

Many phone calls were made during this period. Sami insisted that Jeffrey should come to live with them but of course it was impossible to persuade him. Her cousin's investment in Thailand was total, even though to them it appeared an entrapment.

17th December

Dear Beatrice,

Thanks for your letter and $20
Enclosed my CV and the list.

I can leave it to you to explain about my last two books, how I went unpaid on the Thai book and how the Malaysian book was not published and hence my present financial woes.

If you send money best to do it by "telegraphic" transfer to a bank in Bangkok where it can be drawn by me – ask your bank which Bangkok bank will handle it for them as agents and let me know.

Thanks for all your splendid efforts.

Lots of love,
Jeffrey

P.S. Regarding my contract with the first publisher, it contains a number of perverse and pernicious clauses, one being that if there is litigation or any form of dispute it can only be heard in court under English law. I have no intention of living under English Law as it would means moving back, setting up home and seeking legal aid. So I am not sending you the contract. Better I make what progress I can with the matter here in Bangkok.

On February 1ˢᵗ 1996 Beatrice composed a letter, as Jeffrey's cousin and appointee, sending it to the numerous members of the Whittinghame Club. Enclosed with the letter was Jeffrey's remarkable Curriculum Vitae of published works, works awaiting publication and work in preparation. Included was a list of the innumerable royal ceremonies attended over a twenty-five year period (weddings, coronations, funerals, independence day celebrations etc.) and a further list of the interviews he had had personally with numerous royal personalities. Altogether it was a breathtaking overview of an intense fulfilled life.

Also mentioned in his CV was his immense archive consisting of rare royal genealogies, books, newspaper cuttings, photographs, memorabilia etc; most of which was in Bangkok and some still in England. He even disclosed that some of his Malay papers had been sold to the National Archives of Malaysia in Kuala Lumpur, to cover the cost of his move back to Thailand, explaining that increasing anti-Semitism and anti- monarchist sentiment meant he couldn't stay on indefinitely.

Xmas Card 1995:

with photographs taken by Jeffrey on the lying-in state of the Princess Mother - Grand Palace, Bangkok 15.12.95. He points out the condolence card buried within huge bouquets sent by the Clintons amongst others.

Bangkok, 7ᵗʰ Feb

Dear Beatrice,

Hope you received all the bumpf safely? I expect you're only just returning to normal after the snow! Let me know of any progress you may make – I'm hanging on but time is crucial.

No real news as such. Avoided seeing Narissa at Prince Sanidh Rangsit's cremation last week (Prince Piya's younger brother) – she stayed in London. The King performed the ceremony. Mick Jagger got an honourable mention in the cremation book (Prince Sanidh was very 'jet set' and used to entertain all manner of what in America they sometimes refer to as "Euro trash".

Write soon,

Lots of love,
Jeffrey.

On the back of the envelope was written:-

Many thanks for letter, just received. So far no response to mailing – will keep you informed. Hope you enjoyed Miami.

Beatrice's daughter Daniela had started her first-year university course in Architecture at Miami University in Coral Gables. It was not an ideal choice from a parents' perspective and Beatrice would be journeying down south often to keep an eye on her.

An envelope sent July 1996 containing a small piece of paper without accompanying letter:-

Change of address
From 30th July 1996:-
SAMSEN COURT
105614 Nrakorn Jaisri Road,
Talad Sriyan,
Bangkok 10300. Jeffrey

A sense of deep foreboding assailed Beatrice. Not even a telephone number!

—₥—

Bangkok, 5th November 1996.

Dear Beatrice,

Thanks for your letter. Sorry to hear all the sad family news from England.

Thanks for the article from the Sunday Times – sorry to say there's a fair amount of truth about it. The present reign will be a tough act to follow, mind you its start in 1946 couldn't have been less auspicious, with an anti-monarchist government in power which was either directly or indirectly responsible for the genocide which brought about the change of reign!

The state visit went off marvelously and the Queen and Prince Philip were both in good form and received a rapturous welcome from the Thai people, apart from the warmest greetings from the King and Queen and Royal Family. I managed to get myself into the State Banquet on the first night in the Grand palace and fell prey to attentions of a senior officer from Scotland Yard dressed in white tie and tails. He didn't like seeing a Brit dressed in Thai court dress (my white uniform) and thought he smelt a terrorist rat. He asked me what organization I represented and you should have seen his face when I said

I was freelance! All this took place after the Queen and Prince Philip had arrived and between processions. I was saved by one of the palace staff, a friend, who came up and kept telling me in Thai to keep calm, then led me off to his group of palace officials. Now I know what side I'm really on – the Thai side – and bang goes my O.B.E.! I hope the wretched man checked me up on the Thai Foreign Ministry's list of accredited press as he'd see that my entry on it occupied three lines (they made a point of pointing it out to me when I went to collect my card a few days earlier). But I was particularly peeved as the British Foreign Office, the British Embassy in Bangkok and Buckingham Palace have all no doubt been making free use of my book for this state visit! Whilst all this was going on an elderly dowager collapsed and had to be kept in the Gallery of the Queens for twenty minutes until a stretcher could reach her, although she did have the attention of the King's personal doctor who is always on hand carrying an old-fashioned doctor's bag. I don't know if you saw Whoopi Goldberg's last film "Jumping Jack Flash" in which there was a scene set at the Queen's 'Anniversary Ball' at the British Consulate in New York – well it was exactly like that with everything seemingly going according to plan but all sorts of things going on which shouldn't have been – even the Scotland Yard officer resembled the Consulate official in the film (if you haven't seen it see it, but bear in mind that whilst in the film the Queen wasn't present, in real life she was!).

One final word on the state visit – the Queen thrilled me by addressing the King in her speech at the banquet as "Sir, my brother," thus observing the old diplomatic custom that all reigning Kings and Queens are brothers and sisters, whether or not they are actually related by blood!

The book is all but finished and looks very good. We're just pumping up the picture section so that it is as complete as possible. Then I can rest on my laurels for a while.

Later this week is the momentous Royal Barge Procession, now only rarely performed (I managed to see the last two in 1982 and 1987) and the following week is the cremation of the last surviving daughter-in-law of King Mongkut (Rama 1V) – he was born 1804! That's an amazing genealogical and chronological span. She could have dined out for months in Paris or Rome at smart gatherings referring of "my father-in–law, the late King Mongkut of Siam."

She was 97 and the last wife of Prince Kashemsenta who fathered some seventy–five children, and of course she will be highlighted in the book. By the way her death went totally unnoticed by the Thai people and wasn't even mentioned in the newspaper! (probably because her only son had predeceased her by about fifteen years and in the Thai way she was 'forgotten about').

Lots of love
Jeffrey

P.S. I hope you received my last letter, August/September.

Photos taken by Jeffrey himself of the State Visit were included in his letter.

Another announcement of change of address was received, again no letter, no phone number. It struck terror in the heart of Beatrice.

Change of address:-
From 25ᵗʰ January 1997
Jeffrey Finestone,
Flat 706
Ruen Indra court,
405/2 Arun Amarindra Road
Bangkok Noi, Bangkok 10700

—ᴍ—

An article written by Jeffrey relating to an event that had taken place twenty years earlier was sent to Beatrice around February 1997. It had been printed in the "Bangkok Post. Outlook." (Saturday February 15, 1997.)

There was no accompanying letter.

The title of the article was prophetic: "An Untimely Death" in which Jeffrey stated that the passing of Princess Vibhavadi Ransit was still strongly felt by those who knew her well.

With a team of medics she had visited the most inaccessible regions of Surat Thani, noting the grievances of the villagers and subsequently rectifying them with the authorities

----- It was on one such visit in February 1977 that her helicopter was shot at by communist insurgents.

—ᴍ—

Bangkok, 3ʳᵈ of March 1997

Dear Beatrice,

Thankyou for your letter. I've moved again as you know. And am just finishing off the book ready for publication.

Priya's first (divorced) husband, Prince Jagat of Jaipur (son of the famous Maharani of Jaipur) died suddenly in January in London. The funeral was in Jaipur City and

Priya and the children flew there from Bangkok so things here have been quite hectic!

Things have not improved my end, financially – the book is yet to come out and my advances against future royalties are immense by now. And I haven't decided what to do next! These blockbuster royal books are too time consuming - this took exactly two years. And I have nothing to show for any of it yet. I was interested to hear about the one phone call you had from the sister of the Kadourian brothers. Try and keep in contact with her.

Bangkok gets ever crazier, particularly the traffic and one spends so much time getting about. By the end of each week I've usually crossed the town more than half a dozen times. Luckily I know my way around by now – but to the first time visitor it must be horrendous. Twenty years ago it was just a sleepy Asian city with a military curfew at midnight and dangerous holes in the road.

Priya is going to see Princess Galyani to ask her to do the new forward. This will be the second time and quite an honour if she agrees.

Hope you get to meet the Princess Royal.

Lots of love,
Jeffrey

—ww—

This was Jeffrey's last letter.

Although she had no way of knowing about his imminent demise, the essence of his condition seeped out of the page. She could not admit that her dearest cousin had reached the end. In hindsight it all fell into place and was crystal clear. All efforts to raise money were ignored by the 'old boys'; just one phone call was elicited based on curiosity only.

She had not believed that he 'crossed the town' so often, suspecting that he was in fact seriously ill: a ploy to prevent her from jumping on a plane to help. As it happened even that would not have been possible. Both she and Sami had many problems to deal with not least financial. But, unlike Jeffrey, they had their health and a family with all the worries and joys that involved. The image of his suffering alone, impecunious, without "being in the bosom of family" pierced her heart.

And so, the dreaded phone call reached her domain. It was Robert, calling from Bolivia. She did not have to enquire why he was calling. He never had called before. Jeffrey had passed away Saturday June 28th in a hospital in Bangkok. Although it was July 1st when Robert was informed, the funeral had not yet taken place. Jeffrey had requested to be cremated and his ashes to be scattered in the palace grounds.

Beatrice was beside herself with grief. She sent an urgent fax to the Consulate General in Bangkok. She received an immediate reply on July 2nd, in which the British Embassy offered condolences to both her and her cousin Robert.

They explained that the funeral arrangements were being taken care of by the Princess Mother's Palace, Wang Sa-PaTum: arrangements for the religious rights to be performed at 19.00 hrs on Saturday 5th July and for the cremation to take place at 14.00 on Sunday July 6th. They had been informed by the Palace that it had been Jeffrey's wish to be cremated. The British Embassy had also been informed by the Palace that Jeffrey had written his own obituary the week before to be placed in The Times and The Daily Telegraph in England in the event of his death.

The Pro-Consul went on to inform Beatrice that he believed it would be placed the very same day and that a notice would be placed in the Thai newspapers.

They had sent the contact number for the British Embassy in Bolivia the day before.

Beatrice was requested to inform them of her travel plans should she be coming to Thailand for the funeral in which case the British Embassy would inform the Palace.

It was impossible for Beatrice to make travel arrangements at such brief notice. She was desolate and had an overwhelming desire to talk to Priya. Through well–placed acquaintances she succeeded in obtaining the Princess's home number. Jeffrey had been cremated and his ashes scattered, not in palace grounds as were his wishes, but in the vicinity. "Palace Rules" said the princess. They talked about his illness, which had been simmering for a long time, as Beatrice had surmised. According to Priya, Jeffrey had talked often to her father Prince Rangsit who was given to understand that Jeffrey did not want Beatrice or the rest of the family to know. Nor did he want intervention. The conversation concluded with the promise that she would place his obituary in the two UK newspapers during her upcoming trip to London.

For weeks after, the cousins in England scanned the columns but no one espied any report on Jeffrey. Later, when Priya and Beatrice talked about the publication of the book, she casually mentioned that she had handed over the obituary notice, "But obituaries are so expensive you know. Jeffrey had enumerated my extensive titles, which I just had to delete leaving my simple name."

Jeffrey no doubt would have been anticipating with pleasure the reaction of friends, family and acquaintances reading his notice "Please contact for further info---".

The propriety of enumerating the full title of his publisher, Princess Priya, was of the utmost importance to her cousin, who had lived with vicarious pleasure in the world of royalty for such a long time.

Beatrice wondered whether "noblesse oblige" had been fully implemented.

A letter dated 9th July, was sent by Priya to Beatrice. Enclosed was Beatrice's travelers check with the letter which she had recently sent to her cousin. Priya reported that the check and letter were amongst the things he had taken with him to the hospital where he had subsequently died. She wrote that the cremation had taken place on July 7th. Unfortunately, she continued, Jeffrey had left her a few things to clear up. However, she did say she would miss him greatly describing him as a brilliant writer in his field and also a good friend.

And so it was that the repugnant premonition that had assailed Beatrice in December 1981 came to be realized. A great void appeared in her soul. She had always imagined meeting up one day when they were older, when daily obligations were less pressing, when they could sit together and indulge in stories of times spent together and of the rich anecdotes Jeffrey would have stored up over the years. It was painful to accept the loss.

Epilogue

Initially, within the family, there was a shocked silence.

Then ideas began brewing for a memorial. Robert, from the remote highlands of the Altiplano, had made a suggestion to his cousin Janice. It was a brilliant idea and it was apparent there would be no objections.

Beatrice was astounded to learn that in the early 70's Jeffrey, with his passion for the preservation of old buildings, had saved The Grand Theatre of Blackpool from demolition. In a book written about this momentous event it was stated that there were three key events: and Key Event Number One was initiated by none other than a member of the Victorian Society, Jeffrey Finestone. He had seen the beautiful interior of the Grand and had suggested to the Society that the theatre should be a Listed Building. The Department of the Environment accepted the application and the Grand was listed as Grade Two, a fine example of the work of architect Frank Matcham. The listing was crucial to the campaign to save the theatre in the late summer of 1972, for it meant the Grand could not be demolished without the Minister's permission. In fact, it was reopened in 1981 by none other than Prince Charles!!

By February 1999, a triangle of cousins (Janice in St. Annes, Beatrice in New York and Freda in London) 'huddled together', metaphorically speaking, hatching a plan to celebrate Jeffrey's life and work. Janice had followed up with Robert's suggestion of a memorial plaque in The Grand Theatre of Blackpool and presented this proposal with great enthusiasm and perseverance to 'The Grand Committee'. Not only did they approve unanimously, they also made the wonderful suggestion of placing Jeffrey's memorial plaque at the top of the stairs that led up to the coffee bar and Dress Circle, in an alcove directly facing the Royal plaque. Prominent and unbelievably appropriate!

The date was set: Saturday November 13th 1999.

Janice sent out a letter to all the relatives:-

Dear-----,

When Jeffrey died in 1997 and he was cremated in Bangkok, there was no known grave, and the general idea took form that we might have some kind of memorial for him.

One of Jeffrey's great enthusiasms was the preservation of lovely old buildings, and Victorian ones in particular. When he discovered in the early 70's that Blackpool Borough Council was in the throes of planning to demolish the Grand Theatre and replace it with a Bingo Hall he was horrified, and through his membership of the Victorian Society organized its Listing by the Department of the Environment as a Grade 2 Listed Building.

The huge campaign to "Save the Grand" which was in full swing at the time, has acknowledged that this one single act was a crucial move, and a great turning point for the Grand. The Theatre was eventually saved, and extensively refurbished, being officially re-opened in 1981 by Prince Charles.

It is a most beautiful example of Victorian architecture, and has a wonderful atmosphere and a full & varied programme each year.

Robert came up with the idea of asking the Grand whether we might put up a plaque in Jeffrey's memory, and after a great deal of negotiating we have been offered this honour.

They have asked if we would allow a small short informal unveiling ceremony to give some publicity to the Theatre, and this has been arranged for around 5.30pm on Saturday 13th November, to be followed by a visit to the Ballet performance of Carmen that night, starting around 7.30. This would give us time for a bite to eat and a "get together in between."

If you would like to join us you would be very welcome at the ceremony, and if you could let us know by 30th September whether you are coming, and if you are joining us at the Theatre as well, we can inform them of the numbers they can expect, so that they can reserve free seats for us all.

The cost of the plaque has to be born by the family of course, and should be in the region of 300 pounds. If you could help towards this with a suggested contribution of 30 pounds per family it would be much appreciated. We also plan to give a donation to the Friends of the Grand as a token of our appreciation for their granting this privilege and towards the huge upkeep of the Theatre.

There are only about 3 other single plaques in the entire theatre, so their decision to pay this tribute to Jeffrey was not given lightly!

Yours sincerely, Janice

The response was immediate and complete. All living relatives of Jeffrey in the U.K. were to attend. But Robert, so involved and enthusiastic, found the trip to England with his son Juan Stanley a daunting prospect. Without Robert's presence the dedication would not have been right. Beatrice offered to help her cousin with the plane tickets.

On the Saturday of November 13th all converged on the flat in St. Annes on Sea just one road away from the sea front. A welcoming home, after a refreshing blow on the promenade under a steel grey sky which evoked memories of childhood: the bracing air, the ozone laden briny smell of the Irish Sea and the anticipation of a warm cup of tea in front of the hearth after the 'constitutional.' Janice's living room was filled to the brim with cousins, spouses, offspring and delighted chatter. And how thrilling it was to be in the company of Robert and Juan, now a personable young man with the same easy humour and irony of his father.

Then on to Blackpool, a short drive away, parking the cars and entering into the renovated theatre in all its glory.

The theatre committee greeted them warmly and ushered them up to the Coffee Bar where they were offered champagne. When all guests had assembled they moved to the top of the stairs where the Royal Plaque hung. And opposite was the alcove, covered by a lush red velvet curtain. Silence descended. Everyone understood the honour bestowed upon Jeffrey by placing the acknowledgement of his work directly in front of the Queen and Prince Philip's plaque (which commemorated their visit in 1994). A speech was given by the Chairman of the Theatre Committee. Robert and Beatrice unveiled the Plaque. Jeffrey's presence was palpable. And then the noisy babble of the Beacon clan resumed and they retired to the Coffee bar where a light meal had been prepared for them. Balancing the plates on their laps they avidly caught up on family news. Beatrice's mother, Aunt Ruth and Aunt Edna, the sole representatives of the older generation sat in quiet dignity.

Beatrice's mother was ambivalent about the proceedings: Aunt Freda had been her closest sister and friend and she continued to hold to the belief that Jeffrey had somehow wronged her sister. A ritualistic daily phone call used to be the order of the day and they would murmur happily to each other, Beatrice's mother installed on a comfortable chair in the kitchen, Aunt Freda taking it easy in her bedroom. After her sister died, Beatrice's mother never mentioned her name again. Now widowed for one year, she had retreated into a shell of loneliness and depression. It emerged clearly that she held a deep resentment against Jeffrey, blaming him for her sister's wretchedness at the end of her life. Nonetheless the company of her nephews and nieces livened her up despite her desolation.

They had all been offered Orchestra seats for the evening performance of Carmen, the event of the season. Too excited to leave the family group, only cousin Michael and his wife Valerie chose that option.

The evening came to a close. Reluctantly they left, casting one last look at the magnificent interior of Orchestra and Balcony of the performing space.

Jeffrey had been the subject of a truly Royal acknowledgement befitting his accomplishments. Beatrice hoped his spirit was now at rest.

—m—

Meanwhile, on a random scan of the Internet, Beatrice had come across the critique of a book called 'The Revolutionary King,' the biography of King Bhumibol written around the same period of time that Jeffrey was in Bangkok. A shiver of excitement gripped Beatrice. Unknown forces had guided her to this book review! Even though written at the monarch's request, a British publisher could not sell it in Thailand since Thai laws are so ferocious that people feared if they were associated with the book they could get into trouble. The author, William Stevenson, said that Thais were "scared stiff" that the laws could be interpreted in a "negative way." Stevenson was given six years of access to the King and his family, living in Bangkok and sending his own daughter to the palace school. He said the King, a constitutional monarch, urged him to publish his proposed book abroad as there was otherwise "no way it would ever get past all the guardians."

With some detective work Beatrice managed to find an address and wrote to the author. By November 8th 1999 a reply, postmarked from Toronto, was forthcoming. He knew Jeffrey!

William Stevenson responded enthusiastically. He had known Jeffrey albeit not very well. They would run into each other at the Siam Intercontinental Hotel from time to time, introduced by the hotel public-relations person. He confided that his contacts with the Palace were so hedged around the need for discretion that he was seldom in touch with other Thai nationals. However, he reported that Princess Galyani spoke very highly of Jeffrey's research skills. William continued to explain to Beatrice that he had always thought that it required a dedicated genius to make sense of the most complicated genealogy in the world. His impression of Jeffrey was of a man possessed with tremendous energy whenever he saw him darting through the hotel coffee shop in pursuit of someone he wanted to interview. Unfortunately, he had been asked by the King to keep a low profile while he also tried to piece together His Majesty's remarkable history through his own eyes.

He thanked Beatrice for writing and reassured her she could call or write if she had further specific questions about life in Bangkok

A couple of phone calls ensued wherein Mr. Stevenson patiently explained some of the politics of Thai life and how it was all too feasible for Jeffrey to have been exiled in the manner described. He even admitted that his own life was in peril by having accepted to write about the Thai King.

The saga of Jeffrey's last masterpiece continued.

Another letter from Toronto dated February 2nd 2000 arrived. Mr. Stevenson thanked Beatrice for the material she had sent him on Jeffrey and had exclaimed "what a remarkable man!" He asked if she knew where his papers where and expressed concern that they would be lost, since "the Thais were careless about such documents."

He continued to say that they are somewhat resentful of foreigners who write about them in less than sycophantic terms and believed that Jeffrey would have faced enormous problems.

He also thanked Beatrice for her kind words on his biography of King Bhumipol, regretting that an immense amount of material was left out to avoid giving offense or disclosing matters that must wait a while before they can adequately be dealt with.

—∿—

The book was about to be launched.

On January 30th 2001 The Bangkok Post announced the launch by M.R. Priyanandana Rangsit of **"A Royal Album: The Children and Grandchildren of King Mongkut (Rama IV) of Siam."**

The project was described as a labour of love taking five years done in conjunction with Jeffrey Finestone, who earlier had conducted painstaking research on the royal family for his book "The Royal Family of Thailand: The descendants of King Chulalongkorn."

With the premature death of Jeffrey, M.R. Priya said she was left to edit the book on her own.

The book had been planned as an illustrated family tree covering only three generations (as compared to the other book which covered six generations) since a total of 27 royal lines of descent were derived from King Mongkut as compared to only 15 from King Chulalongkorn. She went on to describe the difficulty of getting the correct ranking and entitlements, more so since it had to be done in both Thai and English.

A book review was published on February 19th 2001 in The Bangkok Post with the heading **"A Royal Feast"**.

The review recognized the importance of Jeffrey's previous book and how it is depended upon for reference into the names and official titles of the descendants of King Chulalongkorn.

Furthermore, it discusses the foreward graciously given by HRH

Princess Galyani Vadhana in which she refers to a book published by HRH Prince Naradhib Prabhandhabongse, listing all the living descendants of his father, King Mongkut. However, the descendants who were deceased before the year 1925 were not listed. With this new publication, she wrote "Jeffrey Finestone has corrected this deficiency---." She added that Jeffreys' death was also a great loss "We have lost in him a writer who could have given us many more books, such as the genealogy of the preceding reigns of the Chakri Dynasty."

The review also included that Jeffrey, in his introduction, had credited M.R. Priyanandana for her friendship and encouragement that allowed him to produce the album.

With over 600 photographs, the review concludes by stating that the book is a valuable source of reference for those who are interested in the genealogy and history of the Chakri Dynasty.

A letter from Priya dated April 24th 2001 thanked Beatrice for her inquiry about the book. She reported it was doing quite well and a lot of PR had made Jeffrey famous again. She included order forms, with the book costing Baht 1,400 (US $ 32) stating that she priced it inexpensively even though it's a hard back. 5000 copies had been printed and she wanted everyone to be able to afford it. However, she added that posting and packaging to USA was expensive and cost an additional 870 Baht.

On July 30th a letter from Priya thanked Beatrice for the cheque. She informed her that she was sending two books by airmail and not charging for the books just the postal fees. A request was made to send the other book to Jeffrey's brother. She reported that the book was selling slowly, but quite well. All the descendants whose families were represented had bought a copy.

Again, she reiterated how sorry she was that Jeffrey wasn't here to enjoy the fruits of his labour.

The books arrived and as Beatrice worried over how to send

Robert's book safely to Bolivia, another magical coincidence occurred. A young man, whose mother she had met in La Paz, one of Robert's private pupils, called her at home. Living in New York, he was on his way to visit his family. Within the week Robert received the book! Beatrice chuckled over the machinations of Jeffrey's spirit.

Bangkok 5th October, 2001; a letter from Priya reported she had received a letter from Robert thanking her for the book. She enclosed a copy of the letter she had written to Robert detailing her suspicions that Jeffrey's first book had been reprinted and was being sold in USA at $250 per copy.

Priya's letter to Robert also involved a detailed discussion of copyright, confirming that Jeffrey had been denied, even posthumously, payment for all his endeavours in Malaysia and Thailand. She describes the first book "The Descendants of King Chulalongkorn" as a masterpiece.

Beatrice made an attempt at Asia House in Manhattan to find out if the Thai book was being sold in the USA but no evidence was forthcoming. For her, and no doubt Robert, it was of little matter. She didn't believe Jeffrey would have wished to pursue that path.

———

And so, the exalted life of Jeffrey has been told and we have reached the end of the tale.

Or have we?

Unable to let go completely, Beatrice searched continuously for more clues that could shed light on her cousin's journey through life. She found an article on April 24th 2003, in which The Daily Telegraph wrote a detailed obituary on D. Williamson, genealogist, co-editor of Burke's Peerage. Jeffrey was described as his young friend and protégé.

"David Williamson and Finestone ——together laid the foundations for the ambitious multi-volume 'Burke's Royal families of the World'——."

Reference to their legendary attendances at Royal Weddings on the Continent is mentioned. But a superficial and heartless description is brushed upon about the court case over the copyright dispute.

By not giving due credit to Jeffrey, the obituary ignored the physical and emotional devastation wrought upon him by this first of betrayals.

The Spring Morning Herald May 12th 2003 (smh.com.au) further elucidates that Williamson and Finestone together broke new ground by tracing all the descendants of George 11.

Beatrice even managed to trace the outcome of **"The Royal families of South-East Asia."** (First noted May 1993 by the Malaysia Tatler).

The publisher Shahindera SDNBHD (Kuala Lumpur) announced in 2002 the publication of the book "The Royal Families of South East Asia" by Jeffrey Finestone and Shahari Talib. Described as a comprehensive guide to the Royal Families of South East Asia, both reigning and formerly reigning royalty, covering Thailand, Laos, Cambodia, Vietnam, Malaysia, Singapore, Brunei and Indonesia.

Each chapter contains a comprehensive photographic and genealogical guide to the families covered as well as brief historical sketches of each family. Lavishly illustrated, as befits its subject matter, the publisher reports that included are detailed family trees decorated with the royal arms of each family. Intended to be an invaluable source of reference to diplomats, politicians and historians.

However, the book is held in two libraries only: one in Australia and one in Thailand. And Beatrice has the 'dummy.' A small consolation.

Photos

Aunt Freda with Jeffrey and Robert

Laotion Embassy Reception / Royal Ascot 1970

The Last Courts
of Europe

Jeffrey Finestone

Introduction by Robert K. Massie

King Ludwig III and Queen Maria Theresia of Bavaria riding through
the streets of Würzburg during a centenary celebration, 1914. Maria
Theresia was also the Jacobite claimant to the British throne, and as such
was regarded by the few remaining legitimists as 'Queen Mary III'.

UK cover

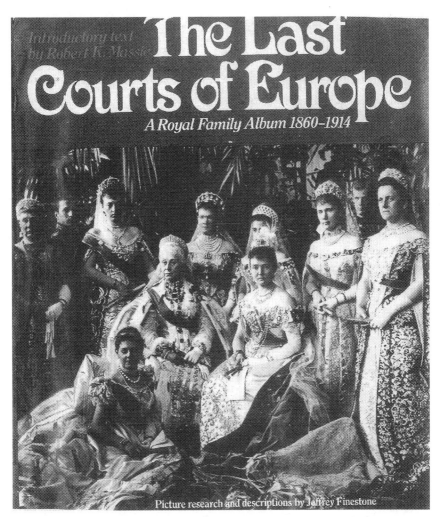

Introductory text by Robert K. Massie

The Last Courts of Europe

A Royal Family Album 1860–1914

Picture research and descriptions by Jeffrey Finestone

USA cover

166

Robert's wedding up in El Alto of the Altiplano in Bolivia 1983

Second book on Thai Royalty published
2001 by MR Priyanandana Rangsit

ผลของการค้นคว้าเรียบเรียงกว่า ๕ ปี - หนังสือ
ลำดับราชสันตติวงศ์พระบาทสมเด็จพระจอม
เกล้าเจ้าอยู่หัวเล่มนี้ เป็นหนังสือเล่มเดียวที่แสดงลำดับศักดิ์
ราชสกุลวงศ์จนถึงชั้นที่ ๓ (ราชนัดดา) พร้อมทั้งมีพระรูปประกอบ
บรรยายพระอิสริยยศและประวัติย่อของเจ้านายสายรัชกาลที่ ๔
รวมทั้งสิ้น ๒๗ มหาสาขา อีกทั้งยังได้รวบรวมพระบรมรูปและ
พระรูปหลากหลายไว้ท้ายเล่ม ทำให้เป็นหนังสืออ้างอิงที่
สมบูรณ์ยิ่งเกี่ยวกับมหามกุฎราชสันตติวงศ์

The result of over five years of labour -
this publication is the only illustrated
family tree showing the complete list of the descendants of H.M. King Mongkut (Rama IV) of Siam ,
up to the third generation. Each chapter provides a
wealth of genealogical details, with a full description
of the ranks and titles as well as portraits of the
King's wives, children, and grandchildren. Rare royal
photographs covering a period of over a hundred
years are assembled so that this book should be an
invaluable source of reference and information on the
Fourth Reign of the Chakri Dynasty.

นายเจฟฟรีย์ ไฟน์สโตน

นักเขียน นักประวัติศาสตร์ และนักลำดับราชสกุลวงศ์
เกิดที่ประเทศอังกฤษเมื่อวันที่ ๑๐ พฤษภาคม ๒๔๙๑
ได้ฝึกวิชาการลำดับศักดิ์ของวงศ์ตระกูลเมื่อทำงานที่สำนักพิมพ์
เบิร์กพีเยอร์เรจ กรุงลอนดอนระหว่างปีพ.ศ. ๒๕๑๕ - ๒๕๑๙ ได้
ศึกษาค้นคว้าเรื่องราวเกี่ยวกับราชสกุลวงศ์ทั่วโลกอย่างลึกซึ้ง
และเป็นผู้เขียนหนังสือ : " คู่มือราชสกุลอังกฤษ " ๒๕๑๖
เป็นผู้เขียนร่วม) " ราชสำนักสุดท้ายแห่งยุโรป " ๒๕๒๔ และ
" จุฬาลงกรณราชสันตติวงศ์-พระบรมราชวงศ์แห่งประเทศไทย "
๒๕๓๒ ผู้เขียนอยู่ที่ประเทศไทยและมาเลเซียกว่า ๑๐ ปี และ
ถึงแก่กรรมที่กรุงเทพฯ เมื่อวันที่ ๒๙ มิถุนายน ๒๕๔๐

Jeffrey Finestone

Author, historian and genealogist, was born in
Great Britain on 10th May, 1948. He received
his early training in genealogy at Burke's Peerage,
London, where he worked between 1972-1976. His
special area of study was the Royal Families of the
world which he researched in depth. His published
books include " Guide to the British Royal Family "
1973 (co-authored), " The Last Courts of Europe " 1981
and " The Royal Family of Thailand-The Descendants
of King Chulalongkorn " 1989. Jeffrey Finestone
spent over a decade living in Thailand and Malaysia and
passed away in Bangkok on 28th June, 1997.

พระนิพนธ์คำปรารภ

ด้เขียนคำปรารภอีกครั้งสำหรับหนังสือลำดับราชสันตติวงศ์ยิ่งเล่มหนึ่ง ในคราวนี้
ของพระมหากษัตริย์ผู้ทรงพระปรีชาชาญพระองค์หนึ่ง คือ พระบาทสมเด็จ
พระจอมเกล้าเจ้าอยู่หัว หนังสือเล่มนี้เป็นผลงาน
เขียน ผู้เชี่ยวชาญในเรื่องการลำดับสายสกุลและเป็นผู้เขียน "จุฬาลงกรณราช
สันตติวงศ์ พระนามพระราชโอรสธิดาและพระราชนัดดา" อันเป็นการลำดับราชสกุลในรัชกาลที่ ๕ จนถึง พ.ศ. ๒๕๓๒ ซึ่ง
ผู้สืบราชสกุลได้ถึงชั้นที่ ๖

พระเจ้าบรมวงศ์เธอ กรมพระนราธิปประพันธ์พงศ์ทรงมีพระชนมายุครบ ๖๔ พรรษา
ภาพสมเด็จพระจอมเกล้าเจ้าอยู่หัวเมื่อเสด็จสวรรคต ได้ทรงนิพนธ์หนังสือเรื่อง
" เพื่อเป็นการเทิดพระเกียรติ พระนิพนธ์ดังกล่าวมีรายพระนามและรายนามผู้สืบ
จอมเกล้าเจ้าอยู่หัวที่ยังมีชีวิตอยู่ในปี พ.ศ. ๒๔๖๘ เป็นที่น่าเสียดายว่าผู้อ่านที่
โอรสธิดา และพระราชนัดดาในพระบาทสมเด็จพระจอมเกล้าเจ้าอยู่หัวอย่างสมบูรณ์
นี้ เพราะรายพระนามผู้ที่สิ้นไปก่อนปี พ.ศ. ๒๔๖๘ ไม่มีปรากฏเลย เจฟฟรี่
ได้หนังสือเรื่อง "สมุดพระรูปพระราชโอรส พระราชธิดา และพระราชนัดดาใน
อยู่หัว (รัชกาลที่ ๔)" หนังสือเล่มนี้จึงจะเป็นประโยชน์และให้ความเพลิดเพลิน
แก่ใจในพระบรมราชวงศ์แห่งประเทศไทย

เจฟฟรี่มิได้มีชีวิตอยู่จนถึงได้เห็นการพิมพ์ตำหนังสือที่เป็นผลงานการค้นคว้า และ
ยศ อีกทั้งยังขอรองให้เขียนคำปรารภสำหรับหนังสือเล่มนี้ในขณะที่เขียน
ไปแล้ว เราได้สูญเสียนักเขียนผู้ที่สามารถจะเขียนหนังสือได้อีกมากมายหลายเล่ม
เช่นรัชกาลต้นๆ แห่งพระบรมราชจักรีวงศ์

กัลยาณิวัฒนา

สมเด็จพระเจ้าพี่นางเธอ เจ้าฟ้ากัลยาณิวัฒนา
กรมหลวงนราธิวาสราชนครินทร์

Foreword

It is a pleasure to write another foreword to a book presenting the descendants of a great king, for
this occasion, King Mongkut, the father of King Chulalongkorn, which again has been researched by the
professional genealogist Jeffrey Finestone, author of the monumental "The Royal Family of Thailand - The
Descendants of King Chulalongkorn" containing the descendants of King Chulalongkorn, down to 1989, year
of the publishing of the volume, until the sixth generation.

In 1925, His Royal Highness Prince Naradhib Prabhandhabongse, upon reaching the age of 64, the
age of his father, King Mongkut, at the time of His death, decided to honour Him by publishing a book with
all the King's living descendants in that year. Unfortunately, the readers who, later on, would have liked to
have the complete list of King Mongkut's children and grandchildren were unable to find it in this book, because
all the descendants, who were deceased by the year 1925 were not mentioned. Jeffrey Finestone has corrected
this deficiency in "A Royal Album - The Children and Grandchildren of King Mongkut (Rama IV) of Siam"
and this book will prove to be very useful and entertaining for researchers as well as for readers interested in
the Royal Family of Thailand.

What saddens me is that Jeffrey has not lived to see the publication of the book that he researched
and wrote entirely, as well as the thought that he had asked me personally to write this foreword while he
was finishing off his book - and now he is no more. We have lost in him a writer who could have given us
many more books, such as the genealogy of the preceeding reigns of the Chakri Dynasty.

Galyani Vadhana

Her Royal Highness Princess Galyani Vadhana,
Krom Luang Naradhiwas Rajanagarindra

Memorial at the Grand Theatre
Janice and Robert
Janice and Robert flanked by committee of the theatre
Beatrice and Robert

Index

Cultural references

p.126 **Blackpool Illuminations**: annual lights festival, founded in 1879 and first switched on 18 September of that year. Held each autumn in the British seaside resort of Blackpool on the Fylde coast in Lancashire. They run from late August until early November.

p.16 **Whittinghame College Brighton**: was a Jewish Boarding school for boys based in Brighton. Founded in September 1931 the school soon prospered. The headmaster and founder was Jacob 'Jake' Halevy (1898-1978).

p.38 **The Living Theatre**: an American Theatre Company founded in 1947 and based in New York City. it is the oldest experimental theatre group in the United States. For most of its history it was led by its founders actress Judith Malina and painter/poet Julian Beck.

p.52 **Les Treteaux-Libres**: an independant theatre company created in Geneva 1967. Formed by Bernard Heymann, Sylviane Fioramont and Jean-Marc Bassoli on the model of The Living Theatre.

p.27 **Chelsea Arts Club**: A private members club on Old Church Street in Chelsea London. Founded 1891 at the height of the bohemian movement in Europe by the American painter James Abbott McNeill Whistler alongside a group of friends. It occupies the same house since 1902.

p.21 **Burke's Peerage:** is a British genealogical publisher founded in 1826 when Irish genealogist John Burke began releasing books devoted to the ancestry of the peerage, baronetage, knightage and landed gentry of the United Kingdom

p.32 **The Sealed Knot:** The Society was founded by a distinguished Soldier and the Country's foremost Military Authority on the Civil Wars, Brigadier Peter Young and a group of friends following a party in Cavalier costume held in the summer of 1968. Over the years the Society has performed re-enactments throughout the country. In 1974 it was granted official recognition as a registered Charity. The Society was granted its own Coat of Arms in1983.

p.35 **Mass held at St. Paul's Cathedral,** London on December 19th 1971 to celebrate the third anniversary the Rock Musical "Hair".

p.44 **The Most Noble Order of The Garter** is an order of chivalry, or knighthood, originating in medieval England. Presently bestowed on recipients in the United Kingdom and other Commonwealth realms: it is the pinnacle of the honors system in the United Kingdom. Membership in the order is limited to the sovereign, the Prince of Wales, and no more than twenty-four members, or Companions.
Established 1348 by King Edward 111.

p.52 **Victorian Society:** Founded in 1958 for preservation and appreciation of Victorian architecture and the arts. Also agreed to have within its remit the Edwardian period up to the outbreak of the First World War.

p.52 **Windsor Festival** (Menuhin and Ashkenazy) Founded 1969 with Yehudi Menuhin and Ian Hunter as Artistic advisors.

Based around the participation of the Menuhin Festival Orchestra using St. George's Chapel, the State apartments of Windsor Castle and other venues around Windsor and Eton.

p.134 **Balkan Relief**

BARF (Balkan Aid Relief Fund) founded 1998.

A group of volunteer Land Rover enthusiasts supplied aid and equipment to the children of war-torn Bosnia Herzegovina.

p.95 **Miner's strike**

1984-1985

a major industrial action to shut down the British coal industry in an attempt to prevent colliery closures.

Opposition to the strike was led by the conservative government of the Prime Minister Margaret Thatcher, who wanted to reduce the power of the trade unions.

The strike was deemed illegal in September 1984 and ended March 1985. It was a major victory for Thatcher and the Conservative Party.

p.108 **Mrs. Thatcher**

b. 1925

d. 2013

Margaret Thatcher; Baroness, LG, OM, DStJ, PC, FRS, HonFRSC, was Prime Minister of UK 1979-1990 and leader of the Conservative party 1975-1990

p.153 **Grand Theatre of Blackpool**

Blackpool Victorian Society p.153

Save the Grand p.153

The Grand Theatre is in Blackpool, Lancashire England designed by Frank Matcham

Opened 1894

Plans were filed for demolition in 1972 but had become a Grade 11 listed building earlier in the year thanks to the initiative of Jeffrey Finestone, a member of the Victorian Society. Unused for three years it was refurbished.

In 1981 the Grand reopened and a Royal Variety Performance was staged in the presence of Charles, Prince of Wales.

Plaque for Queen Elizabeth and Prince Philip at the Grand p.172

p.68 **Broadlands** see: Gerry Famiily

p.18 **<u>Majestic Hotel St Annes</u>**
Built 1909
largest seaside hotel at the time in the country amongst its illustrious guests were Prime Minister Winston Churchill, and many famous stars of the 30's 40's and 50's such as Danny Kaye, Margaret Lockwood, the Marx brothers.
Demolished 1975.

People
(Artists, authors, political figures
and historical personages)

p. 27 **Ley Kenyon:**
b.1913
d.1990

Noted writer, gifted artist and underwater photographer and cameraman.

Captured by the Germans in WW2 he was placed in Stalag Left 111. He was involved in the most gallant escape projects ever attempted by prisoners of war forging documents for the escape. Also he was asked to make a pictorial record sketching under extremely difficult conditions in the tunnel.

In 1951 Jacques Cousteau invited him to dive with him.

In 1960 he taught Prince Philip to dive giving him lessons in the Buckingham Palace Pool.

He was President of the Chelsea Arts Club late 60's, early 70's.

p.68 **Gerry Family**
Eldridge T. Gerry 1744-1814. Signer of the Declaration of Independence and the Articles of Confederation.

p.68 **Broadlands:**
A more than 2,000 acre estate in the foothills of the Catskills. The mansion 'Aknusti' (an Indian word meaning 'expensive proposition') was designed in 1912. Built by Robert Livingstone Gerry, a descendant of Eldridge Gerry. Extensive landscaping by Frederick Law Olmstead's firm was conducted over the course of a decade. The Gerry family retained Aknusti until 1979, when the estate sold the property, fully furnished, to BLF Farms Inc. They operated a thoroughbred breeding outpost.

p.80 **Robert Massie**
> died 12/2/21 at the age of 90.
>
> A Pulitzer Prize winning biographer who wrote immensely popular books on the giants of Russian history: Peter the Great, Catherine the Great, Czar Nicholas11 and Czarina Alexandra

p.77 **Warhol**

p.77 **Lichtenstein**

p.79 **Governor Carey**
> b.1919
> d. 2011
> was an American politician and attorney.
>
> He served as a 7 term U.S. Representative from 1961-1974 as well as the 51st Governor of New York from 1975-1982.

p.75 **Cynthia Lennon**
> b.1939
> d. 2015
> First wife of John Lennon 1962-1968.
>
> Attended Liverpool Art College where Lennon was also a student.

p.73 **Judge Jeffries:** 1st baron Jeffries P.C.
> b.1645
> d.1689
> also known as the Hanging Judge, was a Welsh Judge.
>
> He became notable during the reign of King James 11, rising to position of Lord Chancellor. His conduct as a judge was to enforce royal policy, resulting in an historical reputation for severity and bias.
>
> The 16 words in the U.S. Constitution's 8th Amendment (1791) have their roots in England's Glorious Revolution of 1688-89 i.e. prohibiting against excessive bail, excessive fines,

and cruel and unusual punishments. Descriptions of the grotesque punishments during the reign of King James 11 led to English and Scottish parliamentarians to insist on protections against cruelty and excessive governmental actions.

p.68 Eldridge Gerry

see: the Gerry family

p.65 Pope Pius X

b.1835

d.1914

Pope from 1903 -1914

Known for vigorously opposing modernist interpretations of Catholic doctrine and for his demeanor and sense of personal poverty.

p.65 Al Capone:

b.1899

d.1947

American gangster.

p.65 Rasputin

b.1869

assassinated 1916

a Russian mystic and self-proclaimed holy man who befriended the family of Nicholas 11, the last Emperor of Russia, and gained considerable influence in late Imperial Russia.

A group of nobles led by Prince Felix Yusupov (husband of Princess Irina Aleksandrovina Romanova, the Tzar's niece) concocted a plan to kill him.

He was murdered December 30th 1916.

p.63 Franco and Juan Carlos

Franco

b.1892

d. 1975

was a Spanish general who led the National Forces in overthrowing the second Spanish Republic during the Spanish Civil War. Thereafter he ruled over Spain from 1939-75 as a dictator, assuming the title Caudillo.

Franco decided to name a monarch to succeed his regency.

In 1969 he nominated as heir apparent Prince Juan Carlos de Borbón, who had been educated by him in Spain, with the new title of Prince of Spain.

Juan Carlos 1
b. 1938
reigned as King of Spain 1975 until abdication 2014.

Grandson of Alfonso X111, the last King of Spain before the abolition of monarchy in 1931.

He introduced reforms to dismantle the Francoist regime and begin the Spanish transition to democracy. A constitutional monarchy was established 1978.

p.55 **Ken Russell**
b.1927
d. 2011
was a British Film Director, known for his pioneering work in television and film and for his flamboyant and controversial style.

p.28 **President Amin** *see:* under the country of Uganda

p.88 **Max Karkegi.**
b.1930
d. 2011
historian and great curator of Egyptian history.

he bequeathed to the National Library of France (BnF) a very rich documentary collection consisting of thousand's of photographs and documents on place and personalities of modern Cairo

p.42 **Lord Olivier: Baron Olivier, OM**

b.1907

d.1989

was an English actor and director who, along with his contemporaries Ralph Richardson and John Gielgud, was one of a trio of male actors who dominated the British stage of the mid-20th century.

Oliviers' honours included a knighthood (1947), a life peerage (1970), and the Order of Merit (1981).

p.32 **Lady Aylwen**

Social History London, England. 15th April 1961. Lady Aylwen, wife of Sir George the former Lord Mayor of London, stands around a grand piano with her "actors"- socialites of Mayfair for who she writes surrealist dramas which are performed for one-night audiences for a charge of Â·3,000, never to be performed again, Parts in her plays are eagerly sought after by socialites, A play performed at the Scala Theatre 31 May included "actors" Mr & Mrs Anthony Kinsman, Count Armfeldt and Count de Lasa, The Marchioness of Donegal made the scenery

p.143 **the Clintons**

p.140 **Bismark**

b. 1815

d. 1898

Prime Minister of Prussia 1862-73, 1873- 90

Founder and first Chancellor (1871-90 of the German Empire)

p.135 **Pergau Dam** [Period of discussion 1988-1994]

The Pergau Dam has been called "the most controversial project in the history of British aid"

According to Sir Tim Lancaster, a former British civil servant involved in the affair, the economics of the project was unambiguously bad" since Malaysia could have produced electricity at much lower cost from other sources.

At the insistence of Margaret Thatcher and with the support of her Foreign Secretary, the excessively costly dam was financed with the money of British taxpayers in order to secure a major arms deal.

Britain's attempt to build a vigorous trade relationship with Malaysia backfired on John Major. The Prime Minister was forced to explain why he and his predecessor, Margaret Thatcher, broke official rules on an aid-arms trade linkage.

Dr Mahathir, (4th and 7th Prime Minister of Malaysia), claimed that the newspapers falsely accused Malaysian government Ministers of accepting bribes from British companies. This prompted him to ban all future trade with Britain.

p.108 **Mrs. Thatcher**
b. 1925
d. 2013
Margaret Thatcher; Baroness, LG, OM, DStJ, PC, FRS, HonFRSC, was Prime Minister of UK 1979-1990 and leader of the Conservative party 1975-1990

p.95 **Adnan Khashoggi**
b. 1935
d. 2017
was a Saudi businessman known for his lavish business deals and lifestyle.

Khashoggi was directly involved in helping organize and fund the top-secret Operation Moses in 1984 to airlift to safety

14,000 Ethiopian Jews from Sudan during a famine caused by the Ethiopian Civil war.

p.157 **William Stevenson**
b. 1924

d. 2013

British born Canadian author and journalist.

Invited by King Bhumibol himself to write the story of his life.

He was given unprecedented access to the King and his family

"The Revolutionary King; the true-life sequel to The King and I", was published 1999.

p.125 **Charlie Amatyaku**

Flamboyant Thai culinary guru. Organized the banquet at the Plaza Hotel New York November 1991 for Queen Sirikit.

p.119 **Somerset Maugham**
b. 1874

d. 1965

English playright, novelist, and short-story writer.

He was amongst the most popular writers of his era and reputedly the highest paid author during the 1930's.

During WW1 he served with the Red Cross and in the ambulance corps before being recruited in 1916 into the British Secret Intelligence Service. He worked in Switzerland and Russia before the October revolution in 1917 in the Russian Empiire.

During and after the war he travelled extensively to India, S.E.Asia and the Pacific.

Countries:

1) <u>Ethiopia</u>

p.44 Emperor Haile Salassie 1 of Ethiopia
    b.1892
    d. 1975
    Emperor of Ethiopia from 1930-1974. The heir to a dynasty that traced its origins to the 13th century, and from there by tradition back to King Solomon and the Queen of Sheba.
        He is a defining figure in both Ethiopian and African History.

2) <u>Uganda</u>

p.28 King Freddie Mutesa11
    b.1924
    d. 1969 in UK
    The Kabaka of Buganda, who fled to Britain in 1966 after being deposed as President of Uganda by Milton Obote. After Obote was overthrown in 1971 by General Idi Amin, the new President made plans to bring the Kabaka's body home to Uganda to strengthen his support among the Baganda, the country's largest tribe.

p.28 President Amin
    b. c.1925
    d. 2003
    Ugandan military officer who served as President of Uganda 1971-79. Considered one of the most brutal despots in world history.

p.91 Princess Elizabeth of Toro:
    b.1936

Cambridge graduate, Lawyer, actor, top model, Minister of Foreign Affairs, Ambassador to U.S.,Germany and Vatican in 1960's.

3) Selangor
[see: Palace of the Sultan of Selangor]

is one of 13 states of Malaysia on the west coast of Peninsular Malaysia, surrounding the federal territories of Kuala Lumpur and Putrajaya.

The State of Selangor has the largest economy in Malaysia in terms of gross national product. It is the most developed state of Malaysia with good infrastructure such as highways and transport and has the largest population of Malaysia, a high standard of living and the lowest poverty rate.

p.115 The Sultan of Selangor: Sultan Salhuddin Abdul Aziz Shah Al- Haj (8th Sultan of Selangor)
b.1926
d. 2001
is the constitutional Ruler of Selangor. This position is hereditary and can only be held by a member of Selangor's royal family.

4) Laos

An ancient state, peopled by Thais driven southward from Yunan, in southern China.

The Royal House claims descent from Khoun Borom, the first King of Laos.

A new kingdom known as Lan Xang came into being which prospered especially during the sixteenth century. But the long, elongated geography made unity difficult. In 1695 three kingdoms emerged: Luang Prabang, Vientiane and Champasak.

Between 1898 and 1907 various agreements between France and Siam resulted in the detachment of most of the Lao provinces and their attachment to a French protectorate.

In August 1940, after the fall of France, all Lao territories, west of the Mekong, were returned to Thailand. Japanese troops occupied Luang Prabang in March 1945. With impending defeat of Japan the King reconfirmed the status of the Luang Prabang

An independence movement under the *Lao Issara* established a provincial parliament and deposed King Sisavang Vong Oct 1945.

French troops began reoccupying the country in March 1946 prompting the *Lao Issara* to restore Sisavang Long as King

The country was recognized as a self-governing unit within the French union in 1949. Agents of the Vietnamese communist movement, *Pathet Lao,* emerged.

The next 20 years saw the country in the grip of a three-way bloody contest between the Royal government, the communists and a centre-neutralist faction. Two princes from the reigning Royal family led the Communist faction. The *Pathet Lao* took power between August 1974 and November 1975, forcing the king's abdication Nov 1975. The King, with the Queen and Crown Prince and several other members of the Royal family were removed to "re-education camps" in March 1977. Forced into hard labour they have never been heard of again.

The Lao Royal Family was the ruling family of the Kingdom of Laos from 1904-1975.

p.23 **Crown Prince Vong Savang**
b.1931
d.1979
eldest son of King Savang Vatthna (b.1907 d.1977 or 1984) and Queen Khamphoui (b.1909 d.1982)

5) __Brunei__

A British protecturate since 1888, Brunei seceded from the UK on January 1st 1984

Located on the North coast of the island of Borneo in S.E. Asia.

Separated into two distinct parts by the Sarawak district of Limbang.

The reminder of the island is divided between Malaysia and Indonesia.

The government implements a combination of English common law and Sharia law.

p.95 **the Sultan of Brunei: His Majesty The Sultan and Yang Di-Pertuan of Brunei**
b.1946
is the 29th and current Sultan of Brunei since 1967 (following the abdication of his father) and Prime Minister of Brunei since independence from the UK in 1984.

He is one of the last absolute monarchs in the world.

6) __Penang__: p.108

Prince of Wales Island, The straits settlement

Main constituent island of Malaysian State of Penang. Located in the Strait of Malacca off N.W. coast of Peninsular Malaysia. State capitol is George Town. founded by British East India Co. 1786. Became regional centre for spice production. Briefly occupied by Japan during WW2 before surrendering to Britain. Then merged into Federation off Malaya (now Malaysia)

7) **Trengganu** (Terengganu) p.115

Sultanate and constitutional state of Federal Malaysia.
Emerged as independent sultanate 1724.

In the 19th century became a vassal state of the Thai
Raitanakosin kingdom.

In 1909 power was transferred from Siam to Great Britain.

During WW2 Japan occupied Trengannu and transferred
sovereignty over the state back to Siam, now renamed Thailand
in 1939.

After the defeat of Japan, British control was reestablished.

Tregannu became a member of the Federation of Malaya
in1957, which became Malaysia in 1963.

The Sultan of Terengganu is constitutional ruler of the state
of Tregannu

8) **Sumatra** p.115

one of the Sundra islands of western Indonesia

Largest island that is fully within Indonesian territory.

Proclaimed its independence 1945 and gained independence
from the Netherlands in 1949.

Acts of violence against nobility reached a peak in 1946.

p.115 The Sultanate of Deli still exists but no longer has any political
authority.

Medan is the capital of the Indonesian N. Sumatra Province.

Maimun Palace is a royal palace and is a well-known
landmark. Built 1887-1891 by Sultan Ma'mun Al Rashid
Perkasa Alamyah, the 9th Sultanate of Deli.

Royals

He surrendered his country after the German invasion in May 1940. His act was declared unconstitutional by the Prime Minister who moved with the Cabinet to London to form a government-in-exile.

Leopold and his family were placed under house arrest. In 1944 they were moved to Germany and then Austria before being liberated by the Americans. Banned for some years from returning to Belgium, his brother Prince Charles was declared regent. His eventual return in 1950 nearly caused a civil war and under pressure from the government he abdicated in favor of his son Prince Baudouin in 1951.

Royal Guests and relatives gathered from around Europe for his funeral at the Saint Jacques-sur-Coudenberg Church in Brussels.

p.42 **Empress Zita of Austria**

    b.1892

    d.1989

    Wife of Charles, the last Monarch of Austria-Hungary. As such she was the last Empress of Austria and Queen of Hungary.

Queen Victoria

    b.1819

    d.1901

    Reigned as Queen of the United Kingdom and Ireland 1837-1901, a period of industrial, political, scientific and military change within the U.K. and marked by a great expansion of the British Empire.

    In 1876 the British Parliament voted to grant her the additional title of Empress of India.

    Married in 1840 to her first cousin Prince Albert of Saxe-Coburg and Gotha.

    Victoria's links with Europe's royal families earned her the nickname "the grandmother of Europe".

    Her youngest son, Leopold, was affected by hemophilia and at least two of her five daughters were carriers.

    Through her reign, the establishment of a modern constitutional monarchy continued.

    As Victoria's monarchy became more symbolic than political, it placed strong emphasis on morality and family values.

p.43 **Duke of Windsor:** former King Edward V111.

    The Funeral.

    b.1894

    d.1972

    Great-grandson of Queen Victoria.

    Reigned 20th January - 11th December 1936

    Abdicated December 1936 so that he could marry the American divorcée Wallis Simpson.

The new King George V1 announced he was to make his brother "Duke of Windsor".

He lived in exile in Paris France except when he was Governor of the Bahamas during WW2 (appointed after accusations that he was a nazi sympathizer).

He died at his home in Paris. His body was returned to Britain. The funeral service took place in the St George's Chapel, Windsor Castle in the presence of the Queen, the Royal Family and the Duchess of Windsor.

---

p. 45 **Wedding of Crown Prince of Yugoslavia to Princess Maria da Gloria of Brazil** announced 1971
location: Prince Pedro of Brazil's Palace (outside Seville)
date: 1ˢᵗ July 1972

Brazilian Imperial Family: -
The former Brazilian Imperial Family is a branch of the Portuguese Royal House of Braganza that ruled the Empire of Brazil 1822-89.

The members of the family are dynastic descendants of Emperor Pedro 1.* Dom Pedro)

Claimants to headship of the post-monarchic Brazilian Imperial legacy descend from Emperor Pedro 11, including agnates** of two branches of Orléans -Braganza: the Petrópolis and Vassouras lines. Prince Luis of Orléans-Braganza leads the Vassouras branch.

**agnate: a relative whose kinship is traceable exclusively through males.

Dom Pedro King Pedro 1V of Portugal

* King Pedro 1 of Brazil

b.1798

d.1834

was the founder and first ruler of the Empire of Brazil.

He was the fourth child of King Dom John V1 of Portugal.

When the country was invaded by French troops in1807, he and his family fled to Brazil, Portugal's largest and wealthiest colony.

Pedro's father was compelled to return to Europe 1821 leaving him to rule Brazil as regent. In 1822 he declared Brazil's independence from Portugal and was acclaimed Brazilian Emperor King Pedro 1*

On the death of his father he became King Pedro 1V of Portugal reigning briefly from March 1826 - May 1826 before abdicating in favour of his eldest daughter.

Unable to deal with problems in both Brazil and Portugal he abdicated as king of Brazil 1831 in favour of his son Dom Pedro 11 and sailed for Europe.

bride: **Princess Maria da Gloria of Brazil** p.45

b. 1946

daughter of Prince Pedro Gastão of Orléans- Braganza*

first cousin of King Juan Carlos of Spain.

(*Prince Pedro Gastão of Orleans-Braganza.

b.1913

d. 2007

Head of the Petropolis branch of the House of Orléans-Braganza and a claimant to the defunct Brazilian throne in opposition to the Vassouras branch claim led by his cousins Pedro Henrique and Luis.)

groom: **Prince Alexander of Yugoslavia** p.45

Alexander, Crown Prince of Yugoslavia

also claiming the crowned royal title of Alexander 11 Karadordević.

He is the head of the House of Karađorđević, the former royal house of the defunct Kingdom of Yugoslavia and its predecessor the Kingdom of Serbia.

b.1945

Born and raised in the UK.

Through his father, he is a direct descendant of Queen Victoria through his great great-grandfather Prince Alfred, Duke of Saxe-Coburg and Gotha (Victoria's second eldest son)

Maternally also a direct descendant of Queen Victoria through his great great grandmother Victoria, Empress of Germany (Victoria's eldest daughter).

His godparents were King George V1 and the then Princess Elizabeth, now Queen Elizabeth.

His father, King Peter 11, left his country 1941 to establish a government-in-exile in London.

In November 1945 country was declared a communist republic.

In 1947 all members of Alexander's family except for his grand uncle Prince George were deprived of their citizenship and their property confiscated.

Bride and groom are 4th cousins once removed as both are descendants of Prince Ferdinand of Saxe-Coburg and Gotha (1785-1851).

guests: p 47

: Her Imperial and Royal Highness the Archduchess Robert of Austria

b. 1930

1st child of Prince Amedeo of Savoy and Princess Ann d'Orléans married Robert Archduke of Austria- Este 1953

: Their Royal Highness the Count and Countess of Paris

(see: under the Spanish wedding guest list)

: His Royal Highness the Infante Alfsonso of Spain (the great great uncle of the bridegroom)

: His Majesty King Umberto of Italy
(*see*: under the Spanish wedding guest list)

: Their Majesty King Constantine and Queen Ann-Marie of Greece:-

King Constantine 11
b.1940
Family forced into exile during WW2. Spent his early years in Egypt and South Africa.

Returned to Greece with his family 1946 during the Greek Civil War

His father Paul became new king when King George 11 died 1947.

On the death of King Paul. he acceded king in 1964.

The Colonel's coup on April 1967 led to his fleeing the country in December of that year.

The junta abolished the monarchy 1973.

Lived many years in London, returning to reside in Greece in 2013

Queen Ann-Marie of Greece
b.1946
was Princess Ann-Marie of Denmark, youngest daughter of King Frederick 1X of Denmark.
married Constantine 11 of Greece in 1964

: Their Royal Highness Prince Juan Carlos and Princess Sofia of Spain
(*see*: under the Spanish wedding guest list)

: His Royal Highness Prince Francisco of Brazil
? Francisco Humberto of Orléans-Braganza of the Petropolis line
b. 1956

: Her Royal Highness Princess Ana of the Two Sicilies

:His Royal Highness the Crown Prince of Portugal
(*see*: Spanish Royal wedding list)

: His Royal Highness Prince Paul, ex-Prince regent of Yugoslavia
b.1893
d.1976
Only son of Prince Arsen of Serbia, younger brother of King Peter 1.

In 1934 Paul's first cousin, King Alexander 1 of Yugoslavia was assassinated and Prince Paul took regency until Alexander's son Peter 1 came of age.

Post war Communist Authority in Yugoslavia declared Prince Paul as an enemy of the state banning him from ever returning. His property was confiscated.

Rehabilitated by the Serbian courts 2011.

Reburied 2012 at the family crypt in central Serbia.

: Her Royal Highness Princess Ann*

: Count Adam Zamoyski
b. 1949
Born in New York City
Brought up in England.

His parents, Count Stefan Zamoyski (1904-76) and Princess Elizabeth Czartoryska (1905-89), married in Poland but left their homeland in 1939 soon after its invasion by Germany and Russia.

Oxford educated, he is a freelance historian and author of over a dozen books. Has duel British-Polish nationality.

: Her Imperial and Royal Highness Grand Duchess Valeria of Bade
(niece of Prince Philip by marriage)
b. 1941
Born in Vienna
member of the Tuscan line of the House of Hapsburg-Lorraine and an Archduchess and Princess of Hungary, Bohemia and Tuscany by birth.

Through her marriage to Maximilian, Margrave of Baden, Valeria is a member of the House of Zähringen and Margravine consort of Baden.

: Princess Teresa of Brazil
(see: Spanish Royal wedding guest list in Index)
b.1919
d. 2011
a member of the House of Orléans-Braganza, the 5th and last daughter of Pedro de Alcântara, Prince of Gräo-Pará, disputedly Emperor Pedro 111 of Brazil'

Her nephew, Duarte Pio, is the current claimant for the title of Duke of Braganza and therefore head of the Royal House of Portugal claiming titles, amongst others, King of Portugal.

British Royalty

___

p.33 **Count Nikolai Tolstoy**
b. 1935

British monarchist and historian. He is a former parliamentary candidate of the UK Independent Party and is current nominal head of the House of Tolstoy, a Russian noble family.

His father, Count Dimitri Tolstoy, escaped from Russia in 1920 and settled in the UK.

He is a distant cousin to author Leo Tolstoy (1828-1910)

In 1972, the 'King's Army of the West' was established by Count Nikolai Tolstoy. The Sealed Knot attempted a rapprochement with the 'Kings Army' in 1973. Eventually in 1979 the 'English Civil War Society' was formed as an umbrella organization for the Roundhead Association and the King's Army. Meanwhile the Sealed Knot continued to grow and develop as a unified society.

p.79 **Prince Nikita Romanoff**

b.1923

d. 2007

was a British born, American historian and writer.

He was a member of the Romanov family, great nephew of Nicholas 11 of Russia, the last Tsar.

p.79 **Princess Marie-Loire of Bulgaria**

b.1933

Daughter of Tsar Boris 111.

On Board of Trustees for American University in Bulgaria.

p.62 **Lady Ursula d"Abo**

b.1916

d. 2017

English socialite and aristocrat

Maid of honour to the Queen at the Coronation of King George V1 1937.

p.65 **Duke and Duchess of Windsor**

see also: funeral of the Duke of Windsor p.43

p.65 **Empress Eugenie of France**
b.1826
d.1920
wife of Napoleon 111
Empress of France 1853-70.

p.65 **Prince Felix Youssanoff**
b.1887
d.1967
was a Russian aristocrat.

The Youssanoff family was one of the richest families in Imperial Russia.

Felix led a flamboyant life.

Best known for participating in the assassination of Grigori Rasputin (1916) and for marrying the niece of Tsar Nicholas 1 in 1913.

Exiled, he and his family finally settled in Paris in 1920.

p.65 **Prince Dimitri of Russia** (nephew of Emperor Nicholas 11)
b.1901
d.1980
Nephew of Tsar Nicholas 11 of Russia.

During the Russian Revolution Prince Dmitri was imprisoned along with his parents and grandmother, the Dowager Empress, at Dulber Crimea.

He escaped the fate of a number of his Romanov cousins, who were murdered by the Bolsheviks, when he was freed by German troops in 1919 at the age of 17.

He settled in England.

Following the creation of the Romanoff Family Association in 1979, Prince Dmitri was chosen as its first president serving until his death a year later in England.

p.61 **King Birendra of Nepal**
b.1945

d. 2001
was King of Nepal from 1972-2001.

As the eldest son of King Mahendra, he reigned until his death by assassination.

Enrolled 1959 at Eton College in the UK, he returned to Nepal 1964.

He began to explore the country by traveling on foot to the remote parts of the country where he lived humbly with what was available in the villages.

Later he completed his education at the University of Tokyo before studying political theory at Harvard University 1967-68.

After Mahendra's death in 1972, Birendra consulted his court astrologers, who advised him to delay his coronation for three years, as the the most auspicious moment for his crowning was at 8.37am precisely on 24th February 1975.

The coronation was attended by statesmen and political leaders from 60 nations with the Prince of Wales representing the British Royal Family.

On the auspicious occasion of his coronation, the new king announced that primary education would be free and available for every child.

The 1990 People's Movement was a multiparty movement in Nepal that brought an end to absolute monarchy and the beginning of constitutional monarchy.

Assassination:-
Birendra and his whole family were gunned down by Crown Prince Dipendra (eldest son of the King) at a royal dinner on June 1 2001.

Almost all the royal family were killed except for the younger brother of King Birendra, Gyanendra Shah, who consequently became the king until monarchy abolished 2008.

p.61 **Princess Elizabeth of Schleswig-Holstein**
b.1957

Princess consort to the current head of the Ducal House of Schleswig-Holstein Sonderburg-Glücksburg, Christoph, Prince of Schleswig-Holstein.

p.47 **Princess Anne:** British Royalty
Ann, Princess Royal
b.1950
Second child and only daughter of Queen Elizabeth11 and Prince Philip Duke of Edinburgh

p.58 **Prince Tati of Albania** (Prince of Kosova)
b.1923
d.1993
was the heir presumptive to throne of Albania from the creation of monarchy under King Zog 1 in 1928, prior to the birth of Crown Prince Leka 1939.

p.62 **King Leka 1 of Albania**
b.1939
d. 2011
was the only son of King Zog 1 of the Albanians.

Leka was the pretender to the Albanian throne and referred to as King Leka 1.

King Zog 1 was forced into exile only two days after the birth of the Crown Prince due to the Italian invasion of Albania.

The Royal Family settled in England.

The Albanian Royal Wedding took place in Toledo Spain in October 1975. [King Leka 1 with Queen Susan the first Queen of the world from Australia]

Queen Susan b.1941 d.2004. Strong supporter of her husbands efforts to restore monarchy in Albania.

The Royal Family was invited to return to Albania in June 2002.

p.58 **Prince Rainier's Silver Jubilee**

    Prince of Monaco

    b.1923

    d. 2005

    was the Prince of Monaco from 1949 until his death in 2005, thus ruling the Principality of Monaco for almost 56 years making him one of Europe's longest ruling monarch.

    He was responsible for the transformation of Monaco's economy shifting it from its traditional casino gambling base to its current status as a tax haven and cultural destination.

    In 1956 he married the American film star Grace Kelly*.

    The Silver Jubilee in 1974 celebrated 25 years as monarch.

*Princess Grace: p.58

p.79 **Queen Frederika of Greece**

    b. 1917

    d. 1981

    Direct descendant of both Queen Victoria and Kaiser Wilhelm 11

    Married <u>Crown Prince Paul of Greece</u> 1938, and became Queen on his accession to the throne 1947. Her 23 year-old son Constantine became King after the death of King Paul 1964.

    Lived in exile following the seizure of power by a military junta 1967.

    In 1973 the junta abolished the monarchy

Spanish Royal Family

    King Alfonso 111

    b.1886

    d.1941 in Rome

    Left Spain in 1931 when forced into exile on the proclamation of the Second Spanish republic

Abdicated in favor of his third son <u>Don Juan Count of Barcelona</u> just before his death 1941 (two older sons had renounced their claim to the throne).

Family moved to Rome where they settled in exile 1941 and then resettled to Estoril in Portugal

Infante Juan, Count of Barcelona

b.1913

d.1993

King Juan Carlos 1

b.1938

son of Don Juan Count of Barcelona

appointed to be successor of Franco who deemed Don Juan to be too liberal Ascended to throne on death of Franco 1975.

Married to <u>Princess Sofia of Greece and Denmark</u>

---

p.53 **Spanish Royal Wedding**

location Estoril Portugal October 1972

The ceremony was held in the 16th century Church of Santo Antonio, where 300 guests had gathered.

bride: Infanta Margarita de Borbón,

b. 1939 in Rome

33 year old daughter of <u>Don Juan de Borbón, Count of Barcelona</u> pretender to the Spanish throne and granddaughter of the late <u>King Alfonso X111 of Spain.</u>

Blind since birth. She came with family in 1946 to Portugal. Speaks nine languages fluently and is an excellent pianist.

groom: Carlos Zurita y Delgado, 29 year-old heart specialist from Madrid.

guests: **King Umberto of Italy**

b.1904

d.1983

was the last King of Italy reigning 34 days in 1946.

The only son of <u>King Victor Emmanuel 111</u> who abdicated his throne in favour of Umberto in1944 hoping his exit would bolster the Monarchy.

However, the referendum on the abolition of the monarchy was passed and Italy became a republic 1946.

Umberto lived the rest of his life in exile in Cascais on the Portuguese Riviera. He never again set foot in his native land.

: **The Crown Prince of Portugal** p. 46
[*see* also: Brazilian Imperial family]

b. 1945

<u>Dom Duarte Pio,</u> Duke of Braganza is a claimant to the defunct Portuguese throne as the head of the House of Braganza.

Born in Bern Switzerland he is regarded as a Portuguese national by descent since his father was Portuguese.

His father was the grandson of <u>King Miguel 1</u> (King of Portugal 1828-1834)

His mother was a great granddaughter of <u>King Pedro 1V of Portugal.</u>

In 1950 the Portugese National Assembly revoked the laws of exile from 1834 banning the Miguelist Braganzas and the laws of exile from 1910 banning the Legitimist Braganzas.

In 1951, Dom Duarte visited Portugal for the first time then moved permanently with his parents and brother in 1952.

: <u>former</u> **Queen Joanna** (Ionnia) **of Bulgaria**
b.1907

d. 2000

was third of four daughters born to <u>King Vittoria Emmanuel 111</u> of Italy.

Married <u>Tzar Boris 111 of Bulgaria</u> in 1930.

The Tzar died after a visit to Berlin in 1943. His son Simeon became Tsar and a regency was established led by his uncle Kyril. After the communists took control of Bulgaria 1945, Kyril was executed and the monarchy was voted out of existence.

Joanna fled with her children to Egypt (where her father lived in exile) and later to Spain. She then moved to Portugal.

: Countess of Paris:
b. 1911
d. 2003

was a French-Brazilian memoirist and consort of the Orléanist pretender, Henri, Count of Paris.

Eldest daughter of Dom Pedro de Alcântara of Oréans-Braganza, Prince Imperial of Brazil.

Her father became Prince Imperial of Brazil in 1891 who in 1908 renounced the succession rights of himself and his future descendants to the abolished Brazilian throne.

Princess Chantal:
b.1946
sixth daughter of the Count and Countess of Paris.
Married Baron François-Xavier de Sambucy de Sorgue in 1972. Graduated as a book binder and is now known as an acclaimed artist.

: Dom Duarte Nuno of Braganza (Duke of Braganza)
b.1907
d.1976
Claimant to the defunct Portugese throne as both the Miguelist successor of his father, King Miguel, and later as head of the only Brigantine house after the death of the last Legitimist Braganza, King Manuel 11 of Portugal.

Had three sons, the eldest of whom is Crown Prince Duarte Pio the current pretender of the throne.

: *nearly all* the Spanish royal family:-
Prince Juan Carlos
Princess Sofia
(note in 1975 Juan Carlos ascended to Spanish throne)

:14 members of <u>**the royal family of the Two Sicilies**</u>

<u>Kingdom of the the Two Sicilies</u>: until the Unification of Italy 1861 was the largest, most prosperous, wealthiest and populous of the Italian states.

: <u>Princess Teresa of Brazil</u>
b.1919
d. 2011
a member of the House of Orléans-Braganza, the 5th and last daughter of Pedro de Alcântara, Prince of Gräo-Pará, disputedly <u>Emperor Pedro 111 of Brazil.</u>

    Her nephew, <u>Duarte Pio</u>, is the current held for the title of Duke of Braganza and therefore head of the Royal House of Portugal claiming titles, amongst others, King of Portugal.

: <u>Princess Pia of Brazil</u>
b.1913
d. 2000
daughter of Prince Luiz of Oréans-Braganza and Princess Maria di Grazia of Bourbon-Two Sicilies.

: <u>the Duke of Bourbon-Parma</u> (Robert 11)
b.1909
d.1974
was head of the House of Bourbon-Parma and pretender to the defunct throne of the Duchy of Parma.

June 1944. On Sept 10th 1944 took part in the liberation of Luxembourg

p.43 Queen Liliuokalani of Hawaii
b. 1838

d.1917

Only queen regnant and last sovereign monarch of the Hawaiian Kingdom, ruling from 1891 until the overthrow of the Hawaiian Kingdom 1893.

During the Golden Jubilee of Queen Victoria she represented her brother as an official envoy to the UK.

Ascended to the throne 1891 nine days after her brother's death.

The composer of "Aloha'Oe" and numerous other works during her imprisonment following the overthrow.

Infanta Pilar of Spain
Duchess of Badajoz

Viscontess consort of La Torres

sometimes known more simply as Pilar de Borbón

b.1936

d. 2020

was the elder daughter of Infante Juan, Count of Barcelona and Princess Maria Mercedes of the Two Sicilies older sister of King Juan Carlos 1

She renounced her rights of succession to the Spanish throne when she married a commoner 1967.

Moved with the family to Rome in 1941 and then resettled in Estoril Portugal in 1946.

President of the International Equestrian Foundation 1994-2006.

p.44 Prince Richard of Gloucester
b.1944

member of the British Royal Family

second son of <u>Prince Henry, Duke of Gloucester and Princess Alice, Duchess of Gloucester</u> (*see*: p 180)

youngest of the nine grandchildren of <u>King George V and Queen Mary.</u>

p.43 **King George V1**

b.1895

d.1952

King of the UK and Dominions of the British Commonwealth from 1936 until his death.

Was concurrently the last Emperor of India until 1947 when the British Raj was dissolved.

As second son of King George V, he was not expected to inherit the throne. In 1920 he was made Duke of York.

Married Lady Elizabeth Bowes-Lyon in 1923.

His elder brother ascended the throne as <u>Edward V111</u> after their father died 1936. Later that year Edward abdicated to marry twice divorced American socialite Wallis Simpson.

George became the third monarch in the House of Windsor

p.28 **King Freddie**

see: under country Uganda

p52 **Prince Albert's home**

Prince Albert of Saxe Coburg was husband of <u>Queen Victoria</u>

b.1819

d.1861

born in the Saxon Duchy of Saxe-Coburg-Saalfeld

first cousin of Queen Victoria, he became her consort on their marriage in 1840.

Queen Victoria was so devastated on the death of her husband that she entered into a deep state of mourning and wore black for the rest of her life.

p.46 **Archduchess Rosemary of Austria**

b.1904
d. 2001
born Princess Rosemary of Salm-Salm, daughter of Archduchess Marie Christine of Austria and Hereditary Prince Emanuel of Salm-Salm.
Married Archduke Hubert Salvator of Austria in 1926.
They had 13 children.

p.40 **King of Afghanistan**
Mohammad Zahir Shah; the last King of Afghanistan
b. 1914
d. 2007

State visit to UK December 1971.

Reigned from 1933 until he was deposed 1973.

Serving over 39 years he was the longest serving ruler of Afghanistan since the foundation of the Durrani Empire in the 18th century.

Demonstrating nonpartisanship his long reign was marked by peace in the country that was lost afterwards.

In 1973, while Zahir Shah was undergoing medical treatment in Italy, his regime was overthrown in a coup d'etat by his cousin and former prime minister Daoud Khan, who established a single-party republic, ending more than 225 years of continuous monarchical government.

He remained in exile near Rome until 2002, returning to Afghanistan after the end of the Taliban government

He was given the title Father of the Nation which he held until his death in 2007.

p.40 **Princess Bilquis of Afghanistan**
b.1932
Daughter of King Mohammad Zahir Shah.

In 1959, she and her mother, the queen, supported the call by the Prime Minister Mohammed Daoud Khan for women to voluntarily remove their veil by removing their own.

Accompanied her father on UK state visit in 1971

p.32 **Prince Ali Vassib of Turkey**

b. 1903

d. 1983

was an Ottoman prince.

From 1977 to his death in 1983 he was the 41st head of the Imperial House of Osman, an Ottoman royal dynasty.

After the formation of the Republic of Turkey in 1923 and the abolition of the Ottoman Sultanate and the caliphate the following year, Vassib and other members of his family were forced into exile settling in Nice France.

Permitted to return to Turkey in 1974. From that time he visited annually.

His memoirs have been published in Turkish.

p.32 **Princess Elizabeth of Yugoslavia**

b.1936

member of the royal House of Karadordević

A human rights activist

Former presidential candidate for Serbia

Yugoslavia abolished its monarchy in 1945

p.32 **Princess Dina of Jordan**

(Sharifa Dina bint Abdu'l- Hamid)

b.1929

d. 2019

was a Hashemite princess and the Queen of Jordan from 1955-1957 as first wife of King Hussein of Jordan.

A graduate of Cambridge University and a lecturer in English Literature at Cairo University.

On November 12th 1971 she opened a boutique in Belgravia London, selling Arabic style clothing with profits going to benefit refugee children in Jordan.

p.45 Duchess Barbara of Mecklenberg

b. 1920

d. 1994

Great great granddaughter of Queen Victoria

Married 1954 to Duke Christian Louis of Mecklenburg-Schwerin

Her two daughters are the only remaining senior members of the House of Mecklenburg-Schwerin.

After the death of her brother-in-law in 2001 the House of Mecklenburg-Schwerin became extinct.

p.51 Henry 1V:

b.1553

d.1610

Ruled as Henry 111, king of Navarre 1572-1610 and as Henry 1V, king of France, 1589-1610.

As a Huguenot he was involved in the Wars of Religion. Before his coronation as King of France, he changed his faith from Calvinism to Catholicism. He declared that "Paris vaux bien une messe" ("Paris is well worth a mass").

In 1598 he enacted the Edict of Nantes, which guaranteed religious liberties to the Protestants

p.33 Emperor and Empress of Japan:

Emperor Hirohito:

b.1901

d.1989

Assumed throne on death of his father 1926.

Married distant cousin Princess Nagoko Kuni in 1926

State visit to UK Oct 5th 1971.

It was disclosed that Earl Mounbatten of Burma, former Supreme Allied Commander in South East Asia, who accepted the Japanese surrender there in 1945, did not attend the State Banquet at Buckingham Palace, pleading an undisclosed "former engagement".

p.44 **Emperor Haile Salassie**
see: under country Ethiopia

p 97 **Lord Mountbatten** **(Earl Mountbatten)**
b.1900
d.1979
was a member of the British Royal Family, Royal Navy officer and statesman, maternal uncle of Prince Philip, Duke of Edinburgh, and second cousin once removed from Queen Elizabeth11.

He was the last Viceroy of British India and the first Governor General of the Dominion of India.

Assassinated in August 1979 by members of the Provisional Irish Republican army.

p.94 **Prince Charles**
see: British Royal Family

p.128 **King Bauduin of Belgium**
b.1930
d. 1993
Elder son of King Leopold 111
King of Belgium 1951 until death.
Last Belgium king to be sovereign of the Congo.
Succeeded by younger brother King Albert 11.

p.93 **Princess Elizabeth of Toro**
see: under country Uganda

p.70 **The Royal Wedding** July 29th 1981- Prince Charles and Princess Diane
Married in St Paul's Cathedral London

p.79 **Princess Marie Loire of Bulgaria**

---

p.101 **Dynastic marriage in Rome 1987:** between:-
a European (groom)
Asian royal house (bride)

groom: is son of a Bonapartist pretender to the French throne
i.e. **Louis Prince Napolean***
Paternal grandmother was <u>Princess Clementine of Belgium</u>
b.1872
d.1955
married Prince Napoleon Victor Bonaparte
issue: <u>Louis, Prince Napoleon*</u>
b.1926
d. 1997
Paternal great grandmother was <u>Princess Clotilde of Savoy</u> who was daughter of King Emanuele 11)
b. 1843
d 1911

Also descended from:

Emperor Franz 1 of Austria
b.1830
d.1916
Emperor of Austria, King of Hungary, Croatia and Bohemia and monarch of other States of the Austro-Hungarian Empire 1848 until death.

Leopald 11 of Belgium
b.1835

d.1909

Second King of the Belgiums from 1865-1909 and King-Sovereign of the Congo free State, c characterized by atrocities)

Louise Phillipe1
b.1773

d.1850

King of France 1830-48, the last king and penultimate monarch of France Forced to abdicate after the outbreak of the French Revolution of 1848.

Exiled in the United Kingdom.

George 11
b. 1683

d. 1760

King of Great Britain and Ireland, Duke of Brunswick-Lüneburg and prince-elector of the Holy Roman Empire 1727 until death.

Born and brought up in Northern Germany

Royal Family of Laos
see: under country Laos

p.94 Sultan of Brunei
b.1946

Hassanal Bolkiah is 29th and current Sultan and Yang di Pertuan of Brunei since 1967 and Prime Minister of Brunei since independence from the UK in 1984.

He is one of the last absolute monarchs of the world.

Eldest son of Sultan Omar Ai Saifaddien 111 succeeding to the throne following abdication of his father 1967.

The Sultan has been ranked among the wealthiest individuals in the world.

<u>Independence Day celebration Feb 23ʳᵈ 1984</u>
see; country of Brunei

Royal Family of Deli
see: country of Sumatra

p.132 **Sultan of Pahang** (King of Malaysia 1978-1984)
Ahmad Shah
b.1930
d. 2019
Reigned;1974-2019
was a keen sportsman
Abdication as Sultan was decided by the Royal Council 2019 because of failing health.
Succeeded by his son Abdullah.

<u>Pahang</u>: a large state in Peninsular Malaysia. Known for its mountains, rainforests, and beaches including the white sands and coral reefs of Tioman Island off the east coast.
<u>Pahang Sultanate</u>: was a Malay Muslim state established in eastern Malay Peninsular in the 15ᵗʰ century.

Note: Malaysia Royal Family: Malaysia has unique system with 9 Malay Sultans taking turns to assume the role of King every 5 years.

Largely a ceremonial role, with the Monarch bound to act upon the advice of the Prime Minister and cabinet with few exceptions.

King Jaafar: 10ᵗʰ Yang Di-Pertuan Besar (Ruler) of Negeri Semilan
reigned April 1994-April '99
b.1922
d.2008

Negeri Semilan is an elective monarchy with the ruler elected from male members of the royal family by hereditary chief.

p.137 **<u>Prince Jagat of Jaipur</u>**

b.1947

d.1997

son of <u>Maharaja of Jaipur</u>

ex-husband of <u>Princess Prya Rangsit</u>, the publisher of Jeffrey's second book on Thai royalty

British Royal Family

Queen Elizabeth 11: Monarchical head of State of the UK and 15
   other Commonwealth realms
   b.1926 as Princess Elizabeth of York
   Crowned as Queen on 2nd June 1953.

Prince Philip Duke of Edinburgh: Consort to Queen Elizabeth
   b.1921 as Prince Philip of Greece and Denmark
   d. 2021 as Prince Philip Duke of Edinburgh

Princess Elizabeth of York and Prince Philip of Greece and
Denmark married 1947.
Issue: Charles, Prince of Wales
Ann, Princess Royal
Prince Andrew, Duke of York
Prince Edward, Earl of Wessex

core: carry out royal duties full time :-
Queen Elizabeth
Charles, Prince of Wales
Camilla Duchess of Cornwall
Prince William, Duke of Cambridge,
Catherine, Duchess of Cambridge
Ann, Princess Royal
Prince Edward, Earl of Wessex
Sophie, Countess of Wessex

lower profile; perform some duties:-
Prince Edward, Duke of Kent
Princess Alexandra
Prince Richard, Duke of Gloucester
Birgitte, Duchess of Gloucester

Princess Anne:
Ann, Princess Royal
b.1950
Second child and only daughter of Queen Elizabeth11 and
Prince Philip Duke of Edinburgh

Prince Charles
Prince of Wales
b.1948
Heir apparent
Eldest son of Queen Elizabeth11

Princess Margaret
b.1930
d. 2002
younger daughter of King George V11
only sibling of Queen Elizabeth11

p24 **Royal Ascot**

1711 - Queen Ann first saw potential for a racecourse at East Cote

1744 - Greencoats or Yeoman Prickers formed the Ceremonial Guard for the Monarch at Ascot
Today they offer unrivaled experience to assist guests

1752 - extra entertainment laid on including cockfighting, prize fighting, jugglers etc.

1783 - jockeys instructed to wear the colours of their horses owners
late 18th Century - men in the Royal Enclosure must wear top hats
early 19th Century - dress code emerges

1807 - The Inaugural Gold Cup presented.

1813 - Parliament passed an Act of Enclosure ensuring that Ascot Heath would be kept and used as a race course for the public

1822 - King George 1V commissioned a two story stand to be built in surrounding lawn
Access by invitation only

1825 - The Inaugural Royal Procession begins.:-

: King George 1V led 4 other coaches with members of the Royal Party up the straight mile.
    The tradition continues: at 2pm sharp, each of the 5 days begins with the arrival of the Queen and the Royal Party in horse dawn landaus from Windsor Castle. just 6 miles away. They parade along the track in front of the race goers.

Chakri Dynasty

The Chakri dynasty is the current reigning dynasty of the Kingdom of Thailand.

The family has ruled Thailand since the founding of the Rattanaksan Era and the city of Bangkok 1782.

The Royal House was founded by **Rama 1**: (b.1737 d. 1809), ruled 1782-1809

Rama 11: (b.1767 d.1824), ruled 1809-1824

Rama 111: (b.1788 d.1851) ruled 1824-1851. Died without naming a successor, so his half brother Mongkut took power as Rama 1V

Rama 1V: (b.1804 d.1868) ruled 1851-1868. Mongkut introduced western geography to Siam and a European-style education system.

Rama V: (1853 d.1910) ruled 1868-1910. Chulalongkorn's first reforms were to fight corruption. He sent royal princes to study in Europe.

Rama V1: (b.1881 d.1925) ruled 1910-1925. Vajiravudh started to move towards democracy. He built the Royal Page's College (now down as Vajiravudh College) in the tradition of English public schools. in 1917 he declared war on Germany as an opportunity to promote Siam nationalism.

Rama V11: (b.1893 d.1941) ruled 1925-1935 (abdicated). Prajadhipok was the last absolute monarch and the first constitutional monarch o Thailand.

Rama V111: (b.1925 in Germany d.!946 in Bangkok)) He was never crowned but reigned under regency 1935-1946.He spent a few years in Switzerland and returned to Thailand 1945.He was assassinated in his own bed June 1946.

Rama 1X: (b.1927 in USA, d.2016) Crowned 1946 and reigned until death in 2016. <u>Bhumibol Adulyadej</u> was the world's longest serving head of state and the longest reigning monarch in Thailand. He was highly revered by the Thai people.

Thai Royals

p.137 **King Mongkut** (Rama1V)

b.1804

d.1868

Initiated the modernization of his country, embracing Western innovation.

Best known through the publication of the memoirs of Anna Leonowens who taught the children of King Mongkut from 1862-1867. Adapted, via a fictionalized version, into the 1951 musical "The King and I".

p. 105 **King Chulalongkorn** (Rama V)

b.1853

d. 1910

his reign was characterized by the modernization of Siam, governmental and social reforms, and territorial concessions the British and French.

p.136 **King Vajiravudh** (Rama V1)

b.1881

d.1925

Reigned 1910 -1925

Succession Law passed 1924: code for Chakra dynasty:-

the throne would be passed to the king's sons and grandsons

The law gave priority to the children of his mother Queen Saovabhan Phongsri over the King Chulalongkorn's two other royal wives

The law also forbade princes whose mother was foreign from the throne. This referred to his companion Prince Chakrabongse who had married a Russian woman. His son Prince Chula Chakrabonse was barred from the throne,

King Vajirayudh had no sons. Thus, the throne would pass to his eldest "true "or full brother

Prajadhipok in 1925.

Note: **King Prajadhipok** (Rama V11)

    b.1893

    d.1941

    His reign was a turbulent time for Siam due to political and social changes during the Revolution of 1932

    He is the only Siamese monarch of the Chakra Dynasty to abdicate.

    He was 33rd and youngest son of King Chulalongkorn.

    He soon found himself rising rapidly in succession to the throne, as his brothers all died within a relatively short period.

    In 1925 he became absolute monarch at 32 years old. Crowned King of Siam 1926.

    Had no children.

    Abdicated 1935 to be replaced by his nephew Ananda Mahidol.

    Spent the rest of his life with Queen Rambhai Barni in England.

    Being the last remaining son of Queen Saovabhan, the crown went back to the sons of the queen whose rank was next to hers, Queen Saving Vadhana. Her son Prince Mahidol, although deceased, had two living sons: Ananda and Bhumibol.

Note: **King Ananda Mahidol** (Rama V111)

    b.1925

    d.1946

    date of burial 1950

    eighth monarch of Siam from Chakri dynasty as Rama V111

    At the time of his recognition as King he was a 9 year-old boy living in Switzerland and was allowed to complete his studies there.

    He returned to Thailand 1945. Six months after his return, in June 1946, he was found shot in his bed.

p.157 **King Bhumibol** (Rama1X)

see: Biography of King Bhumibol by William Stevenson, "The Revolutionary King' published 1999

b.1927

d. 2016

Highly revered in Thailand.

In 1992 played a key role in Thailand's transition to a democratic system.

Succeeded by son Vajiralongkorn (Rama X)

p.126 **Queen Sirikit**

queen consort of King Bhumibol

b.1932

married 1950

p.133 **Princess Galyani of Vadhana of Thailand**

King Bhumibol's sister.

b.1923 in England

d. 2008

Wrote the Forward to both books by Jeffrey on the Thai Royals.

p.139 **Princess Mother**

Princess Srinagarindra

King Bhumibol's mother

b.1900

d.1995

of Thai-Chinese descent, Sangwan Chukramoi had lost both her parents by the time she was 9 years old.

Taught to read by her mother she was sent to live with a relative who was a nanny to a daughter of King Chulalongkorn (Rama V).

When 13 years old was enrolled in Midwifery and Nursing at Siriraj Hospital

Selected to further her studies she was offered a scholarship to the U.S.A.

On a group visit of Thai students to Boston she met <u>Prince Mahidol Adulyadej</u>

<u>Prince Mahidol</u>: The Prince Father b.1892
d. 1927
married 1920 to Sangwen Chukramoi
issue: Galyanij Vadhana
Ananda Mahidol (Rama V111)
Bhumibol Aduyadej (Rama1X)

Regarded as the father of modern medicine and public health in Thailand
Founded the House of Mahidol or the present Royal Family of Thailand.
69th child of <u>King Chulalongkorn.</u>

Prince of Chai Nat: (Rangsit Prayurasakdi)
Prince of Jainad
b.1885
d.1951
son of <u>King Chulalongkorn (Rama V)</u>
Thai founder of the Public Health Ministry.
Appointed <u>Regent</u> while King Bhumibol was finishing his education

sons: Piyarangsit Rangsit
Sanidh Prayresakdi Rangsit

p.111 **Prince Piyarangsit Rangsit***
b.1913
d.1990
Brother of Prince Sanidh.
Children: _
Mom Rajawongse Yaovalaksana Rangsit b.1938

Mon Rajawongse Vibhananda Rangsit b.1947
Mon Rajawongse Priyanandana Rangsit b.1952*

p.148 **Princess Vibhavadi Rangsit :**
b.1920-1977
d,1977
(House of Chakra)
Married HSH Prince Piyarangsit Rangsit
Mother of Priya.*

Inherited her father's gift for writing and became a well-known writer under her pen name V.na Pramuanmarg.

Died in an attack by communist insurgents. The helicopter, in which she was trying to bring two wounded border patrol policemen hospital in Surat Thurn, was shot down.

p.144 **Prince Sanidh Prayurasakdi Rangsit:**
Brother of Prince Rangsit
b.1917
d.1995

p.137 **M.R. Priyanandara Rangsit** *
b. 1952
daughter of Prince Piyaransit Rangsit*and Princess Vibhavedi Rangsit granddaughter of the Prince of Chai Nat married Maharaja Sawai Man Singh 11 of Jaipur

Editor and Publisher of Jeffrey's last book *"Royal Album.The Children and Grandchildren of King Mongkut (Rama1V) of Siam"* published 2000.

Narissa. Mom Rajawongse Narisa Chakrabongse.
b.1956
Thai publisher, author and environmental activist.

Published Jeffrey's first book on Thai Royalty *"The Royal Family of Thailand: The descendants of King Chulalongkorn,"* published 1989.

Only daughter of Prince Chakrabongse and his English wife Elizabeth Hunter. Her paternal grandfather was Prince Bhuranath, (son of Rama V).

Founder and CEO of River Books.

With her aunt Eileen Hunter she authored "Katya and the Prince of Siam," a biography of her Ukrainian grandmother.

p.147 **Prince Kashemsanta ;** Son of Rama 1V.
Fathered 75 children
b.1856
d.1924

Royal Events

p.147. **Royal Barge Procession:** in Bangkok, November 1996
For Royal Kathin Ceremony at Wat Arun
Religious and royal significance, a traditional Buddhist festival
Has taken place for nearly 700 years.

In the reign of King Bhumibol 16 royal Barge processions were conducted the last being The Royal Kathin ceremony at War Arun which was scheduled for October 2011 but postponed because of massive flooding. Run on 9th November 2012.

Books and Articles published

Guide to the British Royal Families: coauthored
: published 1973
Renamed "Burke's Guide to the British Royal Family" omitting Jeffrey's contribution.

The Last Courts of Europe published 1981

Jeffrey Finestone collected photographs over several years from many sources around the world. Many came from the private albums of European royal families and have never been seen before; others were found in archives of State libraries or contemporary illustrated magazines. They cover state occasions as well as the domesticity of home life. There are photographs of the Tzar's Coronation in Moscow which was being recorded on camera for the first time, and of royalty at play in the resorts they frequented.

In edition, Jeffrey wrote short descriptions of all the royal courts flourishing in Europe from 1860 to 1914, when the Great War brought most of them to a tumultuous end.

Dimitri, Prince of Russia (not found as a publication)

The memoirs of Emperor Nicholas 11's nephew.

Jeffrey was co-author with the late Prince Dimitri, Prince of Russia.

Borneo Bulletin March 3 1984: p.89

Article on Jeffrey noted how the late Lord Mountbatten had assisted him in his quest to write about the British Royal Family

The Royal Family of Thailand: The descendants of King Chulalongkorn: published 1989

Foreword: by <u>Her Royal Highness Princess Galyani Vadhana of Thailand</u>:-

"————-Jeffrey Finestone takes us into the extremely complicated system of royal rank and titles of Thailand - perhaps the most complicated in the world.

Even though the kings of former reigns were absolute kings, who could promote a prince to any rank they chose, they still obeyed strict rules that Jeffrey Finestone understands better than many members of our Royal Family————"

Jeffrey first visited Thailand in 1977 for the wedding of Their Royal Highnesses Crown Prince Maha Vajiralongkorn and Princess Somsavali. He returned in 1982 for the Bicentenary Centennial celebration of the Chakri Dynasty and again in 1985 for the cremation of her Majesty Queen Rambai Barni.

He first began gathering genealogical information on the Royal Family of Thailand in 1971 and has, over the years, maintained contact by meetings and correspondence with members of the Royal Family, thereby becoming a world authority on this fascinating subject.

The Bangkok Post: Saturday February15 1997, Outlook

Article on Princess Vibhavadi Rangsit written by Jeffrey commemorating her untimely death 20 years earlier.

Malaysia Tatler November 1990: Jeffrey's article on W. Somerset Maugham p.114

—ɯ—

A Royal Album: The Children and Grandchildren of King Mongkut (Rama 1V) of Siam. (published 2000)

Foreward: by Her <u>Royal Highness Princess</u> <u>Galyani Vadhana,</u> <u>Krom Luang Naradhwas Rajanagarindra.</u>

It is a pleasure to write another forward to a book presenting the descendants of a great king, for this occasion, King Mongkut, the father of King Chulalongkorn, which has again been researched by the professional genealogist Jeffrey Finestone, author of the monumental "The Royal Family of Thailand- The Descendants of King Chulalongkorn".

In 1925, His Royal Highness Prince Naradhib Prabhandhabongse, upon reaching the age of 64, (the age of his father, King Mongkut, at the time of his death) decided to honor Him by publishing a book with all the King's living descendants in that year. Unfortunately, the readers who, later on, would have liked to have the complete list of King Mongkut's children and grandchildren were unable to find it in this book, because all the descendants, who were deceased by the year 1925 were not mentioned. Jeffrey Finestone has corrected this deficiency in "A Royal Album-The Children and Grandchildren of King Mongkut (Rama V) of Siam" and this book will prove to be very useful and entertaining for researchers as well as for readers interested in the Royal Family of Thailand.

What saddens me is that Jeffrey has not lived to see the publication of the book that he researched and wrote entirely, as well as the thought that he had asked me personally to write this forward while he was finishing off his book - and now he is no more. We have lost him as a writer who could have given us many more books, such as the genealogy of the preceding reigns of the Chakri Dynasty.

In anticipation of publication Jeffrey wrote in 1996:-

On my return to Thailand in 1994 after a prolonged and involuntary absence of some six years, it took me a long time to decide what to turn my attention to. Many people, particularly members of the Royal Family, presumed that I would naturally write about the family of King Mongkut (Rama 1V). However, at first I held back due to certain memories connected with my previous book "The Royal Family: the Descendants of King Chulalongkorn". Also, I was unwilling to take on the task of writing a full Rajasantatiwongse (or complete list of descendants) of King Mongkut, which, apart from being very time consuming would have meant a book considerably bulkier than my Rajasantatiwongse of King Chulalongkorn.

Although it is not usual for a writer to publicly thank his publisher with an acknowledgement (and something I have never done before), I would on this occasion beg to be allowed to thank my new publisher, Mom Rajawongse Priyanandra Rangsit, the daughter of my late friends Prince Piyarangsit Rangsit and Princess Vibhavadi Rangsit, not only for the hand of friendship she held out to me on my return to Thailand, but also for finally persuading me to seriously consider writing about King Mongkut's family, which we decided in the Thai way, to limit to the first and second generations in descent from His Majesty, i.e. his children and grandchildren. I would also like to thank her for making it such a short and easy production.

During the writing of this book, much of which took place in the year 1996, a year of unparalleled royal ceremonial in Thailand with the State cremation of her Royal Highness Princess Sri Nagarindra the Princess Mother and the Golden Jubilee of His Majesty the King, many unknown or unclear facts about the immediate family of His Majesty King Mongkut emerged, particularly concerning the longevity of some of his closest relatives. At the time of writing the book there were still two daughters-in-law of King Mongkut living in Bangkok, that is of a man born in 1804! There were also, among his immediate family, three living centenarians, a granddaughter and two granddaughters-in -law, two of whom have since died. The first of these, Mom Knew Voravarn na Ayudhya, widow of His Serene Highness Prince Nityakorn Voravarn, died on the day of a total eclipse of the sun over Thailand, on October 24th, 1995 - and the second, Her Serene Highness Princess Vimalamas Kashemsanta died on June 10th, 1996, on the day of the Golden Jubilee of His Majesty the King. Both royal ladies, as well as King Mongkut's last surviving official daughter-in-law, Mom Bien Kashemsanta na Ayudya, widow of His Royal Highness Prince Kashemsanta Sobhagya, Prince Brahma Varanuraksha, who died on September 12th, 1996, received the royally ignited flame from the King at their cremation in Bangkok.

Links between the descendants of King Mongkut and the Court are still very strong and many of his grandchildren and great-grandchildren can be seen at royal ceremonies, some attending on a most regular basis. Seven Princes and Princesses, grandchildren of King Mongkut, took part together with other more senior members of the Royal Family, in the Brahmanical ceremony of Vien Then (the passing of lighted candles of allegiance) which was performed in the presence of His Majesty the King in the Chakra Maha Prasad Throne Hall of the Grand Palace, Bangkok, during the Golden Jubilee ceremonies of June 1996.

Some years ago I was lunching with the late Prince Prasomsvasti Sukhasvati and he told me that when he was in the United States and was asked to explain just who he was he used to reply, with a touch of understatement, "one of the many grandsons of King Mongkut of Siam", a remark which at the time it was made covered a group of about one to two hundred Princes. Today such a remark could only be made for a group of some 17 Princes and 23 princesses and former princesses. The eldest living grandchild of His Majesty King Mongkut, Her Serene Highness Princess Bongse Bismayakashemsanta, was born in 1900, the eldest grandson, His Serene Highness Prince Charunriddhidej Janankura, who was born in 1932 and the youngest granddaughter, Her Serene Highness Princess Meri Svastivatana who was born in 1932.

There are some twenty-seven royal lines of descent (Rajasakul) from King Mongkut (twenty eight if one includes the line of descent of King Chulalongkorn, the so called Fifth Reign Rajasukul), all but one of which received separate surnames from King Vajiravudh (Rama V1). The only one not to receive a surname from His late Majesty was the family of Prince Gagananga Yugala, Prince Bijit Prijakorn, who received their surname of Gagananga na Ayudhya from King Prajadahippok (Rama V11) on June 29th, 1929. Some of the Rajasakul are very extensive - Prince Kashemsanta Sobhagya, Prince Brahma Varanuraksha, had over seventy children and this family, the Kashemsanta family, together with the Devakul and Svastivatana families are among the largest families, which today number several hundred members apiece. Other families, such as Gagananga and Vadhanawongse are relatively small.

Jeffrey Finestone
Bangkok, December 1996/2539

—॥॥॥—

The Royal Families of South East Asia: by Jeffrey Finestone and Prof. Shaharil Talib (published 2002)

This unique publication is a comprehensive guide to the Royal families of South-East Asia, both reigning and formerly reigning royalty, covering Thailand, Laos, Cambodia, Vietnam, Malaysia, Singapore, Indonesia, and Brunei.

===

236

Archives:-

European Royalty : request author for information
Thailand and South East Asia: Princess Prya Bangkok
Malay papers: Malaysian National Archives

Author: Barbara Schofield Suleiman is a British born retired pediatrician and geneticist. She lives in New York City with her husband, a playwright. Currently editing her husband's plays and fiction.

Printed in the United States
by Baker & Taylor Publisher Services